P9-ARU-992

Hélène Cixous

University of Nebraska Press: Lincoln and London

Verena Andermatt Conley

Hélène Cixous:

Writing the Feminine

Portions of Parts 1 and 2 have previously been
published, in different form, as "Writing the Letter:
the lower-case of hélène cixous," *Visible Language*
12(Summer 1978): 305-18; "Missexual Misstery,"
Diacritics 7 (Summer 1977): 70-82; and "Cixous
and the Uncovery of a Feminine Language," *Women
and Literature* 7 (Winter 1979): 38-48.

The paper in this book meets the guidelines
for permanence and longevity of the Committee on
Production Guidelines for Book Longevity of the
Council on Library Resources.

Library of Congress Cataloging in Publication Data

Conley, Verena Andermatt, 1943-
Hélène Cixous: writing the feminine.

Bibliography: p.
Includes index.
1. Cixous, Hélène, 1937- —Criticism and inter-
pretation. 2. Feminism in literature. I. Title
PQ2663.I9Z6 1984 848'.91409 83-23600
ISBN 0-8032-1424-3 (alk. paper)

I do not want to tell a story

to someone's memory.

Hélène Cixous

For T.

Contents

ACKNOWLEDGMENTS

This study was aided by a grant from the National
Endowment for the Humanities in 1980 and by an
Alumni Grant from Miami University. I would like to
thank Hélène Cixous, who has shown continued
interest in the research and has given timely
suggestions in its elaboration. Because little of her
work has appeared in English, all translations from
the French are mine. One section of the first part and
two of the second originally appeared in *Visible
Language, Diacritics,* and *Women in Literature.* I
wish to thank those journals for allowing me to
reformulate some of the material beyond its original
conclusions. My thanks to Marguerite Sandré for
helping me with some of the unpublished material.

Chronology of Hélène Cixous

1937 Born in Oran, Algeria. (Her father died while she was very little. Her mother's family is of Austro-German descent, and Cixous's mother tongue is German.) 1958 Birth of her daughter. 1959 *Agrégation* in English. 1961 Birth of her son. 1962 *Assistante* at the University of Bordeaux. 1965–67 *Maître assistante* at the Sorbonne. 1967 *Maître de conférence* at Nanterre. Publishes her first text, *Le Prénom de dieu*. 1968 Docteur ès lettres. Doctoral thesis: *L'Exil de James Joyce ou l'art du remplacement*. With Gérard Genette and Tzvetan Todorov, founded the review *Poétique*. Appointed *Chargé de mission* to found the experimental University of Paris VIII at Vincennes. 1968– Professor of English Literature at Paris VIII-Vincennes, now at Saint-Denis. 1969 *Dedans* awarded the Prix Médicis. 1973 With *Portrait du soleil,* started to write specifically about the question of sexual difference. 1974 Established the *Centre de recherches en études féminines* at Paris VIII. 1976 Started publishing all her work at the Editions des femmes to show her political commitment to, and participation in, the women's movement. 1982 Stopped publishing at Des Femmes in order to enjoy greater poetic freedom, which, she felt, had been reduced by pressures and interpretations of the relation between the poetic and the political. 1983 *Promethea* published by Gallimard. **Decisive readings:** Shakespeare, Joyce, the German Romantics (especially Kleist, Kafka). Philosophy (Kierkegaard, Heidegger, Derrida). Freudian Psychoanalysis. The poets (Rimbaud, Rilke). The Brazilian writer Clarice Lispector.

Hélène Cixous

1

Textual Strategies

May 1968: student-worker uprisings, the occupation of the Sorbonne—a stronghold of outworn pedagogical traditions. Intellectuals cast aside their differences and march in the streets. Their demands: new universities; improved curricula; access to schools for everyone, not just for the privileged few. The political ferment is paralleled by an intellectual ferment with the advent of the human sciences, and readings in philosophy, psychoanalysis, anthropology, linguistics. It is a period of belief in the revolutionary power of language and of hopes for a shattering of millenary oppressive structures. Women want their share. They rally behind the banner of "liberation" in teaching, criticism, writing. Twenty years after the publication of Simone de Beauvoir's *Second Sex,* women in search of a new feminism continue their readings of Freud and Marx, to whom they add others. They read new theoretical works in and about major discourses governing society in an effort to determine how and where women have been excluded and how to question and undo that exclusion.

It is not my intention here to establish a historical determinism, or to link such a historical "event" to such a cultural "event." I simply want to read some of Cixous's writings, published roughly since the May uprisings in 1968, the period of the founding of Vincennes, the founding of the *Centre de recherches en études féminines* in 1974, and her temporary involvement with the MLF,[1] followed by a new departure, away from an official political affiliation. In these fifteen years, a writing of enthusiasm and effusive energy appears almost mensually. It is here, during that time and in those rhythms, that I situate the pages to follow.

Subversion through Poetry

Cixous comes to writing via fiction. A collection of short stories, *Le Prénom de dieu,* is published in 1967. In 1969, *Dedans,* a fictional autobiography about her entrapment in an oedipal scene, is awarded the Prix Médicis and catapults her to the fore of the Parisian literary scene, which she has occupied ever since. She publishes her 900-page doctoral thesis, *The Exile of James Joyce,* in 1968. Her radicalism spills over the boundaries of a narrowly defined feminism. As an Algerian, Jew, and woman, she finds herself thrice culturally and historically marked and vows to fight on all fronts against any form of oppression. One of the founders of France's furthest left university, Paris-Vincennes (Paris VIII)—now moved for political reasons to the suburb of Saint-Denis—she was been conducting seminars on writing, femininity, and sexuality over the last decade. Though there is a shift in her work from a covert to an overt "feminism," Cixous has always been interested in the inscription of the feminine in text and society.

A longstanding French tradition believes that art is necessarily "to the left," on the side of subversion of existing "bourgeois" values. In the wake of the rise of human sciences, moreover, Cixous asserts that social structures cannot be dissociated from linguistic structures. Language, far from being an atemporal tool, is inextricably linked to history and society. Its structures define and constitute the subject. There are no absolute, immutable values beyond words or the grammar and syntax that order them. To change existing social structures, the linguistic clichés that purvey them and make them appear as transparent, immutable truths must be detected, re-marked, displaced. Hence Cixous's interest in language and its use in artistic practices.

First and foremost a writer, Cixous considers poetry—defined not in opposition to prose but as the subversion of coded, clichéd, ordinary language—necessary to social transformation. For Cixous as well as for many other writers, poetry condenses, renders opaque, carries greater psychic density. It is opposed to discourse that flattens, systematizes.

Most important for her definition of the feminine is the fact that Cixous does not proceed on a purely conceptual level, though she dialogues with concepts of philosophy and psychoanalysis. While her texts alternately emphasize one over the other, Cixous, like other modernists, questions the distinction between theory and practice. Her poetic texts are more a theoretical praxis; her critical and her pedagogical readings at Paris VIII emphasize the theoretical. As a result of her own resistance, little of her theoretical work has been published except for *Prénoms de personne,* "Sorties" in *La Jeune Née, La Venue à l'ecriture,* and a number of articles in *Poétique, New Literary History, Signs.*

As a writer, Cixous engages by definition in a solitary, narcissistic (selfish) activity. Writing keeps the other out, physically, and presupposes leisure time as well as an income. An individualistic activity, writing may nevertheless bring about some changes in others' perceptions of the world. One should not, therefore, confuse levels nor let oneself be indicted by tribunals where one does not belong. A writer is not a lawyer or a guerrilla-woman. In a collective endeavor, each fights in her own way, with her own medium, according to her talents and a freedom of choice dictated to some degree by economics and geography. Cixous's concerns are political, but textually political, and she states the premises (and limits) of her enterprise: to read and write texts in order to displace the operating concepts of femininity in major discourses governing (Western) society. In this she is close to other "feminists"—Julia Kristeva, Luce Irigaray, Sarah Kofman—as well as male thinkers: Jacques Lacan, Gilles Deleuze, but mainly Jacques Derrida, with whom Cixous from her specifically (*féminine*) literary border, maintains an ongoing dialogue.

The Loss of the Self

The French attempt at a feminine writing has its equivalent in the United States, where women advocating the expression of a self abound. Writers like Adrienne Rich praise feminine experience in poetry and prose, while critics like Kate Millett expose its exclusion through (male) sexual politics in criticism and fiction. But whereas the former work is based on the importance of an experience lived and felt, on the expression of a self, the latter proposes a loss of subjectivity and ego, a plural self always already other, as well as an erasure of the division between life and text, between before and after. This is not to say that there is no experience; quite the contrary. But there is no experience prior to its enunciation in and through language. This is most important for Cixous, who, following psychoanalysis, believes in speech that enables her to do the economy of her desire, to "traverse" an experience. There is always room for something to be desired, yet this desire is not based on lack. The insistence is on movement, not stasis. Speech is never all rational, scientific. Always becoming, it never becomes the system, the recipe to be applied. Conflating poetry and politics, reading and writing, from what she calls a feminine border, Cixous has been the major proponent of a writing of the feminine or a feminine writing.

Like that of other feminists, Cixous's writing attempts to break away from cultural stereotypes, essentializing concepts and their attributes such as man/woman, masculine/feminine, active/passive. She tries to displace the conceptual opposition in the couple man/woman through the very notion of writing and bring about a new inscription of the feminine. Simone de Beauvoir had written from the vantage point of an existentialist humanist: "*On ne naît pas femme, on le devient*" (one is not born woman, one becomes woman). Similarly, though less humanistically, Cixous questions the traditional concept "woman" defined by its predicate *passive* and shows how what appeared as an immutable concept was part of a historical moment, that of logocentric (Western) thinking, privileging the concept, presence, truth, and making possible our idea of paternity, the father/son relation, and the repression of woman.

Philosophy with Psychoanalysis

In her classes at Paris VIII, Cixous insists on what is of importance in all her writings, as in anybody's writings. She does this via a quotation from Derrida's *Dissemination:*

> A text is not a text unless it hides from the first comer, from the first glance, the law of its composition and the rules of its game. A text remains, moreover, forever imperceptible. Its laws and its rules are not, however, harbored in the inaccessibility of a secret; it is simply that they can never be booked in the *present,* into anything that could rigorously be called a perception.
>
> And hence, perpetually and essentially, they run the risk of being definitely lost. Who will ever know of such disappearances?
>
> The dissimulation of the woven texture can in any case take centuries to undo its web: a web that envelops a web, undoing the web for centuries; reconstituting it too as an organism, indefinitely regenerating its own tissue behind the cutting trace, the decision of each reading.[2]

In Derrida's remark "a text remains imperceptible," one must listen to the etymology of im-per-cept-ible, from *captio,* to capture, to take, the very *cept* of the con-*cept.* The imperceptible of the text is that which cannot be arrested, which remains elusive. There is no hidden secret to be revealed, no truth to be extorted, but there is always that part of the text, the imperceptible, the writerly, the unconscious dimension that escapes the writer, the reader. Even an attempt to reconstitute what an author "really meant" (*vouloir dire*) comes back to saying only "what I meant when my reading crossed this text, on this day, at a certain hour."

Reading then is writing, in an endless movement of giving and receiving: each reading reinscribes something of a text; each reading reconstitutes the web it tries to decipher, but by adding another web. One must read in a text not only that which is visible and present but also the *nontext* of the text, the parentheses, the silences. Silence is needed in order to speak, to write. One phoneme differs from another phoneme, and in speaking, a voice traces, spaces, writes. There is no true beginning; writing is *always already* there, as Derrida said, adopting and making famous a Heideggerian expression. This critique of the origin, of the paternal capitalization, of the castratory gesture of an *à partir de,* a "from there, from then on," is essential. It questions authority (of the father). It opens onto *differance*—not a concept, not even a word, but the movement of something deferred or of something that differs, escaping an assignation, a definition. *Differance* does not have a punctual simplicity, that of the *point,* the period, of the *sujet un,* identical to itself, an author-head-god. What passes from one language to another, from one sex to another, in translation, is always a question of *differance.* Sexual *differance* replaces difference; movement supersedes stasis and Hegelian differences recuperable into dialectics. Derrida insists on the differential between masculine and feminine as both, neither one nor the other, where one signifier always defers the other. He undoes paternal authority, in Cixous's words, from a "masculine border," yet does not broach the possibility of a maternal, a matrical. This is where *her* work "begins."

Such a philosophical reading and writing already questions and displaces the truth of its genre through recourse to psychoanalysis. Yet the real analytical contribution comes from Lacan. Freud, notes Cixous, had recourse to literature, but his readings differ from ours. Freud thought of the text as a product of the author, as a verification of the writer's neuroses, as a process of identification. Freud was interested in the signified. The work of art had a hidden message to be deciphered. Cixous praises Lacan, who was able to show through a double contribution by contemporary linguists, Ferdinand de Saussure and Roman Jakobson, how a signifier always refers to another signifier in an endless chain. With help from Freud's *Interpretation of Dreams* and Jakobson's theory of language, Lacan was led to establish the two poles in language: that of condensation, substitution, metaphor, or symptom, and that of concatenation, metonymy, or desire. Combined with Saussure's readings of the anagrams in Latin poems where the name of a general is reinscribed through letters and phonemes, this opened the way to a different analytic reading practice, away from themes and signification. In her classes Cixous stresses what her texts perform, a philosophical *and* analytical reading, one that combines both dimensions but without attempting to enclose the world in its discourse, as a kind of total analysis. To this must be added a reading on the semantic level, a graphico-phonic reading, which listens to silences, looks at graphic tracings.

Cixous reads and writes at the interstices of Lacan's theory of language—that of the chain of signifiers and not that of the phallus—and Derrida's *differance*. She focuses on reading and writing from a feminine border, not from the between, which for her is too much of a masculine position. She attempts to displace further Derrida's "masculine" displacement toward what she will come to call a feminine economy.

Until now, the majority of writing has fallen under the phantasm of castration, a masculine phantasm which some women under pressure have interiorized. Writing has always been done in the name of the father, and the question must be asked, how do women write? What are the effects in artistic productions of the inscription of their desire?

For Cixous, the terms "masculine" and "feminine" do not refer to "man" and "woman" in an exclusive way. A clean opposition into man and woman would be nothing but a correct repression of drives imposed by society. Cixous writes (of) sexual *differance* from her feminine poetic border in dialogue with a certain philosophy and a certain psychoanalysis. She searches poetically for operating concepts of femininity and economies of sexual difference(s) that would not come back to unity and sameness.

Cixous carries out her call to writing, and her production is abundant. Aware of the violence of our gesture, of the *coup de dé,* the dice throw of our *de*cision, we *de*cided to "begin" reading her ongoing questioning of femininity around different strategic moments, where text and biography engender each other, flow into each other:

1. Cixous's dialectics of excess, an exuberant practice for the limitless as social liberation, based on readings by Georges Bataille, Nietzsche, Hegel; critical articles collected in *Prénoms de personne;* an article on character in fiction; the writing of the limitless in *Le Troisième Corps, Commencements, Neutre;* a questioning of the law (of the father) and a re-traversing of her North African origin in *Portrait du soleil;* a rewriting of one's name in a neo-Joycean work, *Partie.* Cixous meditates on the possibility of social changes through writing and, like other new novelists, on the transformation of narrative.

2. *La Jeune Née, La Venue à l'ecriture, LA, Souffles.* Cixous calls on women to break their silence, to write themselves, to explore their unconscious. She develops the notion of a "bisexual" writing around Freud's Dora. *Angst* marks the passage toward a writing to and from the woman.

3. *Vivre l'orange, Illa, With ou l'art de l'innocence, Limonade tout était si infini.* Cixous's (belated) discovery of a Brazilian woman writer, Clarice Lispector. From the insistence on a rewriting of the Hegelian desire of recognition, the emphasis shifts toward a Heideggerian problematic of the approach of the other and the calling of the other. Though not advocating separatism, Cixous writes more from and toward the woman. This move is accompanied by a temporary shift from established publishing houses like Grasset and Gallimard to Des Femmes. Cixous discards the notion of bisexual writing and develops her theory of libidinal economies.

The Question of the Canon

Cixous, like other French writers, does not limit her critique of logocentrism to an a priori gender distinction but, on the contrary, reads male authors who exceed dialectics, who are "singers of spending and waste," who transgress limits and inscribe feminine libidinal effects. There are women who write on the masculine side and men who do not repress their femininity. We should note that in France, feminist readings are not equivalent, as much as in the United States, to "opening the canon." Feminist readings all question a certain type of logocentric or phallogocentric discourse that may be used by men and women alike. It has been used predominantly by men because of historical and cultural circumstances. The "canon" as it exists in American English departments does not have its exact equivalent in France, where reading and writing do not necessarily go through university channels and where an academic affiliation is not a prerequisite to intellectual success. Rather, the question of the canon is linked to social classes. There has always been a conflictual coexistence of several literatures and literary histories, Communist, Catholic, and maybe an official academic one. Throughout the century, iconoclasts—dadaists, surrealists, existentialists, and new novelists—have been busy questioning what they referred to as "bourgeois tradition." In a French tradition, letters and politics are seldom separated, and letters are usually thought to be on the side of subversion—at least since the French revolution.

French writers have been wanting to shock the bourgeoisie (to which they also belong) since that class came into power. Recently, Sartre's existential literature has not observed the rules of "le beau," of aestheticism or decorum; adepts of the new novel dehumanized what they called the traditional novel—anthropomorphic, ethnocentric—by "decentering" man and putting him within objects. Cixous's writings are part of a long chain which, from nineteenth-century poets to new novelists, attempts to question the values of bourgeois art. Cixous, like many others, defies the very language on which these values are founded. As an institution, literature reinforces the values of the dominant class. The literary establishment serves a class interest under the guise of moral and aesthetic values. Literary discourse must marginalize itself not through socialist-realist techniques but through the questioning of language. Cixous does not address the question of bringing literature to the masses, presupposing that anyone can read anything at all times and that accusations of hermeticism usually come from educated readers. She does, however, following May 1968, question the connection between literary establishments and pedagogy, and it has to be noted that many of the participants in her seminar are working women and foreign students.

Cixous writes at the interstices of fiction, criticism, psychoanalysis, and philosophy without enclosing herself in any of them. Mocking a certain academic approach to "literature" as a "rite of passage" into culture, a rite through which a ruling social class integrates itself into a symbolic mode, she urges a different literary reading/writing. Writing is not the simple notation on the page; life-and-fiction, life-as-fiction is one of unending *texte* (or *sexte*). Cixous does not privilege an economy of death, which she sees inevitably linked to conservatism and unity of self. She emphasizes an affirmation of life, movement, exuberance.

Absolute knowledge represses the senses, effaces signifiers and the body in order to accede to an idealized signified and the spirit; textuality based on originary repression eroticizes writing, questions the sign and its binary structure. In Cixous's writing of the feminine, subversive practices intervene on multiple levels: on a material level (phonemes and graphemes), on a conceptual level (questioning of the concept), and in an ongoing reflection on writing. The real she wants to transform is never a natural real, is never separated from language. Such a writing, we have said, calls for different reading practices. Reading and writing are not separate activities. A text is always guilty, in an Althusserian sense. A text is a rereading, not only because we must reread in order not to consume but also because it has already been read. We approach it with the memory of other texts, and there is no innocent reading as there is no innocent writing.

For Cixous, all writing is necessarily "autobiographical," and in each text there are unconscious dimensions. "Consciously," from *Dedans* to *Limonade tout était si infini,* Cixous writes texts of transformation and addresses the problem of writing as a woman, from a writing of the feminine to a feminine writing. In the pages to follow, it will be a question of reading Cixous's texts from the angle of sexual *differance,* in their movement, in their *cheminement.* The insistence of recurrent motifs grouped around woman, body, law, writing, is evident. We chose not to group these motifs but to read them in an ongoing (re)writing of the scene of sexual *differance.* We decided to read the texts around certain strategic moments of writing the feminine, in its play with other feminines, other masculines, and ask in turn questions of textual economy. This leads at times to extensive quoting, a repetition which is not a duplication. The necessity of quoting also derives from the urgency to "present" many of the texts unavailable to the English-speaking reader in an effort to give breadth to Cixous's *oeuvre* beyond "The Laugh of the Medusa" and *La Jeune Née.*

2

Beyond a Coincidence of Opposites: The Step of the Gradiva

Cixous comes into life, is born, through writing. For her, to write *is* to live. Writing is always a question of life and death, a question that has its corollary in another: who wants my death, who wants me to die? or, who wants me to live and love? To a (metaphoric) death—castration—of the other, Cixous opposes love and affirmation of the other. Desire undoes absolute knowledge, reason, mastery; decapitates (paternal) authority; divides the origin, the "I," as a dramatically autonomous machine overtakes authorial control of language. In these early texts it is a question of the limitless, of (impossible) births, of beginnings, of the inscription of a feminine. Yet the writing scene is still in the shadow of the father.

Desire of Intensity: *Prénoms de personne*

In a collection of essays, *Prénoms de personne,* Cixous reads fictional texts that question the unity of the subject, authority, and inscribe sexual difference. Written in the early seventies, at a time when the novelties of theories outdid underlying divergences, and before the splintering into groupuscular units, the essays draw from Lacan, Derrida, and Deleuze, all of whom inform the writing of Cixous's own philosophy of fiction. The title, *Prénoms de personne,* does not confer meaning upon a body of text that follows. The anagrammatization of *père* into *pré, per,* dismembers the (paternal) body. *Prénoms:* first names, not last names that would inscribe the subject into a patrilinear genealogy, a plurality of first names, multiplying the effects of the subject; and *pré-nom,* that which is before the noun, before something is named, given unity. *Personne,* as both somebody and nobody, *Pèresonne,* Joyce's Noboddaddy, remains undecidable. *Prénoms de personne* theorizes Cixous's position(s) on fiction and criticism through a reading of literary texts. The loss of one's name, the divisibility of the self, the inscription of masculine and feminine are read in Freud, Kleist, Joyce, Hoffmann—all part of Cixous's "canon"—and others then known on the Parisian literary scene, like Poe.

The opening sentence has the ring of a manifesto: "I ask of writing what I ask of desire: that it have no relationship with the logic that puts desire on the side of possession, acquisition, consummation-consumption [*consommation-consumation*] which, so gloriously pushed to the end, links (mis)knowledge with death. I do not think that writing—as production of desire, where desire is capable of everything—can be, or has to be, defined through the border of death."[1] The tone is that of infinite belief in transformations, in a freeing of the individual from social constraints and laws. Cixous is close to Deleuze, who states in *Logique du sens* that there is no logic of meaning. Implicitly, Cixous rejects the paradigm of Hegelian desire from *The Phenomenology of Mind* as it manifests itself in the master/slave rapport. Desire of death is at the same time a desire of unity and totality. Cixous does not go beyond the affirmation of a simple rejection of the paradigm, nor does she elaborate the notion of desire. The instancing of the "I" with its implicit second person "you" (in)directly addresses the reader in dialogue—a constant in Cixous—and puts a strong autobiographical element into her critical writing.

The Eradication of Death

Cixous's concern is to affirm life and eradicate (metaphoric) death. She writes: "Death is nothing. It is not something. It is a hole. I can fill it with phantasms and give it a name, if I want. I can also think castration, but nothing human or real obliges me to do so. Nothing can prevent me from thinking otherwise, without taking death into account. It will be a question of limitless life, of all life in these texts: a question, I say, for they all have in common this question which they answer in various ways, of the possibility of something limitless [*d'un sans-limite*]."[2] Effusive, on the side of exuberance and abundance, the displacement of limits is an opening toward an infinite, toward a limitlessness. *Bord* and *hors:* a border, limit, and its outside. Writing concerns itself with "what is happening in this non-locus [*non-lieu*] that cannot really be described, presented, and that the word fiction designates to inscribe a troubling, moving adventure beyond genres and oppositions, where the real is not defined by its contrary, where the literary is not an emanation of something else to be printed, where a phantasm is not simply filling a gap, where desire is not a dream, where, in the *plusreal,* the elsewhere to come announces itself."[3] The political gesture of writing consists in pushing back death and its phantasms. Already, in these early texts, there is a tendency to equate death with the masculine and life with the feminine. In *Prénoms de personne,* Cixous is concerned with a desire of intensity that would replace a desire of appropriation based on the death of one of the partners. This summit of desire, of height—close to Bataille's notion of sovereignty which, beyond a simple coincidence of opposites, displaces Hegelian mastery—inscribes itself in the functioning of a *writing* that exceeds the logos. The furtive, gliding moment is one of appeasement and love, where selves have been shed and overtaken (*dépassés*). Sovereignty has to be read outside of hierarchies, as that which rids itself of quotidian preoccupations, obstacles, closures, possibilities of reversal, on the side of spending, the gift, and birth.

Across her readings of Freud, Kleist, and others, Cixous wants to read "how, when, and where I hear that my reading relates me to the real the way I wanted to transform it. For me fiction, which is an action, has an efficacity."[4] Fiction privileges life. It is action insofar as it opens new possibilities through meaning as well as through textual play. It functions as a subversion of repressive, political constraints that limit and control the imagination. Eradication of death and its (unconscious) representations—a death reversible into life in a limited economy and not that death which, paradoxically, is an affirmation of life, of risk—is necessary to transform social and affective economies based on property, being, and the law. This transformation will open the space of the gift, of positive loss and spending in a general economy not reversible into gain.

The Space of the Gift

The problematic of the gift became popular in France in the late forties when, through the texts of Claude Lévi-Strauss and secondarily of Simone de Beauvoir and Georges Bataille, attention was drawn to Marcel Mauss's *Essai sur le don.* Mauss focuses his anthropological research on the gift as a means of communication and exchange in primitive societies. In particular, he mediates on customs of ritualistic potlatch practiced by some Northwest Indian tribes. Mauss sees the destruction of fortunes during ritual as an improductive use of wealth, one based not on exchange but on a loss radically different from our Western notion of *troc* and economic exchange tied to capitalism, accumulation, and gain. During potlatch rituals, a chief may destroy huge quantities of goods (or men), and the other chief, in more spectacular fashion, will have to outdo him. Rivalry is not limited to possession but consists in the sumptuous, gratuitous, playful destruction of fortunes. The poor serve the rich, who, however, cannot consume their fortunes behind walls as in later capitalism. Fortunes are there to be wasted. The gift leads to spending rather than to accumulation, though there is still a possibility of gain in social status. Bataille, taking off from Mauss's efforts to combine anthropology and sociology, criticizes the latter for advocating what he nevertheless thinks to be a normalizing function of the gift and proposes a possibility of spending, of *dépense,* that would undo all rationality and would inscribe itself in a general—not limited—economy underpinned by laughter.[5] There, culture as a system of exchange challenges notions of author, literature, boundaries between disciplines, and inscribes concepts of philosophy in an intense, emotional discourse. It is in the interstices of Bataille's writings—and Derrida's readings of him—that we must read many of Cixous's early texts.

Since affective economies are always related to political and social economies, a civilization based on spending and loss would not suffer from the hard, censuring, anal constraints reflected in the desire of recognition of our own civilization.[6] For Cixous as well as for others, the gift as excess, as spending and abundance, becomes, because of her cultural position in (Western) society, woman's essential attribute; because she has always been repressed culturally, she is more capable of giving than man.

In *Prénoms de personne,* Cixous throws out a call to struggle on two fronts: subjectivity and intersubjectivity. The affirmation of the divisibility of the subject is not distinguishable from a critique of intersubjectivity, of the rapport between masculine and feminine, man and woman, vitiated by the threat of castration, petty anti-life speculation (*le petit calcul anti-vie*). Sexual economy based on castration and death limits the possibilities of life, furthers gain, far from the space of the gift. Economic exchange is linked to recognition and debt as social contract. A change in sexual economy calls for another logic, one that will bring about eroticism without lesion.

Reading/Writing at the Summit

"Another logic" is inseparable from new reading and writing practices. Reading is always double: "Insofar as the literary text speaks about something, as literature is a means to travel *toward* the signified, and insofar as fiction is a new way of inventing new meanings, the text is thinkable through a double operation: I read it with the help of a critical, philosophical reflection and push it to the threshold where its novelty seduces and unbinds me [*me délie et me délit:* to unbind and to unread from the known, to take out of the bed]. I want to read at the summit, where the hope and the necessity to change the world, life, the subject, engender summit-texts [*font pointer les textes-cimes*]."[7] The reader/writer is unbound at the crossing of the unconscious dimensions of the text and her own unconscious. *Délie,* once the name of the absent woman in Sceve's torturous poems, has splintered into a multiple shading of readings in lower case with Mallarmé (and Derrida): *délit,* the crime dividing the idea; *l'idée,* the play between a masculine *délit* and a feminine *idée, el(le), il,* the letter *i, l'i,* and the more graphic *L i,* the open square.

To carry out a literary-philosophical (analytical) reading raises questions of life and death: What makes some people push back death in life? What are the economies of a text? Cixous turns to texts that "shake the ground"—or the classical division between figure and ground—and tarnish mirrors. She urges work on the signifier *and* parallel work on the signified, a dialogue between literary effects and philosophical (analytical) concepts.

She finds those subversive literary practices mainly among the German Romantics:

Literature has long been at work at the subversion with which one embellishes it today. In pre-Marxist and pre-Freudian times, before the conjoined efforts of psychoanalysis and of linguistics, of anti-idealism, had radicalized the deconstruction which is now taking its course actively and massively, the same struggle existed in different forms, in different ways: it was done more violently and more desperately, *à texte nu,* less subversively and more offensively. For the German Romantics, the same bastions had to be destroyed as for us. Logocentrism and idealism, theology, all supports of society, the structure of political and of subjective economy, the pillars of property. The repressive machine has always had the same complicities, homogenizing reason, reductive, unifying which has always allied itself with the master, the unified subject [*sujet un*], stable, socializable. It is there that literature has always struck, at the basis, where these theses and concepts of order imposed themselves. It denounced them at the level of the signified. Well before Bataille, Kleist, and Hoffmann had made the trial of Hegelian idealism, of the cloturing dialectic of recognition. Those poets were singers of spending and waste, against conservative narcissism; they tear the subject away from subjugation to the self, the proper, dislocate the puppet, cut the threads, and trouble mirrors.[8]

A Theater of Eyes

Subversive, these poets are also givers of force and form. Effracting the literary ground, they produce astonishing effects of *sortie* (exits, departure). *Sortie,* a key word in Cixous, insists on excess, on the *passage* out of a system, always toward the other. It stresses movement more than the fact of being on an outside (which would be death), a movement which privileges the ear more than the eye. All these poets must be read from the uncertainty of a *double-entendre* (a double meaning). Romantic fiction, dealing with dream and anxiety, is close to analysis. Significantly, it is a reading of Freud's *Uncanny,* a text between analysis and literature, that opens *Prénoms de personne.* Cixous stresses the attraction that literature held for Freud, who recognizes his debt. Analysis is interested in the psychic life, in the deep areas, and is therefore envious of the creator. "The secret, the enviable power of the creator who succeeds in seducing us, that is what fascinates Freud."[9] The analyst's envy of the creator confirms Cixous's own belief in a certain literary absolute. Yet she is critical of Freud's distinctions between form (or prime of seduction) and content (or real *jouissance,* bliss) and mocks his reduction of literary material to analytic certainty which, for her, always occurs at the point of elimination of the feminine.

Most readings in *Prénoms de personne* approach the questioning of limits between self and other, masculine and feminine, from the angle of the daughter, Cixous's own position in her early writings. In Hoffmann's *Sandman,* the main character is not a woman, but there is a story of a daughter, the divine doll Olympia, who, as automaton, reaches absolute perfection. She is the father's doll, fabricated and kept alive by him, who has a key to rewind her. Everyone knows that Olympia is a mannequin except for the son, who can see only under the authority of the father, the eye of the law.

Olympia, as the father's daughter, reaches the limit of divine perfection and ravishes the eye, yet she is death-in-life. The story, about (the secret of) femininity, is that of a dismembered body—Olympia—over which two fathers quarrel.

Cixous critiques Freud's reading of Ernst Jentsch's analysis of the story. Freud displaces Jentsch's analysis from Olympia and intellectual uncertainty about her as real or mannequin, as fiction or reality, to an adequation: Coppola = Coppelius. A simple paronomasia reduces intellectual uncertainties to a rhetorical certainty. Freud can install analytic truth at the point of elimination of Olympia, or the feminine, and of focalization on Nathanael, or the male. He occults the disquieting figure of the sandman in an easy association, sandman = loss of eyes = castration, and thus reduces Hoffmann's theater to some rigid formulation. There is no writing of fiction without psychoanalysis, and writing is always a product of the unconscious, but analytic concepts must be written out and not simply used as concepts. Poetic writing exceeds analysis; it is more complex because of its use of language. The unscientific literary text escapes final truth and easy allegorization. Fiction, far from being unreal, is "another" form of reality, enigmatic and uncanny. Uncanniness never quite disappears; it "represents" that which in solitude, in silence and obscurity, will never be presented to us: neither real nor fictitious, "fiction," secretion of death, anticipation of nonrepresentation, hybrid, body composed of language and silence which, in the movement that turns it and that makes it turn, like a puppet, invents doubles and death.[10]

In her own reading of *The Sandman,* Cixous, haunted by the law, by the urgency to displace its limits, proposes a theater of the eye, one of substitution and reflection. Decapitating the paternal authority, Cixous writes as daughter, from a divided origin, with a hollow paternal phallus. Such a writing is still linked to the eye, traditional model of knowledge, but it insists, with Freud and Nietzsche and Marx, in a certain sense, on everybody's camera obscura, away from timeless truth. Playing on its own theatricality, its *mise en scène,* such a writing represents nothing but itself. The reader looks through fissures and cracks with glasses that double her sight and complicate mirrors. There is no look from the outside, no truth. The reader is urged not to be content with a role as spectator but to jump into Nathanael's circle of fire, to become "another" reader, to keep a certain magic, a certain mysterious quality. To prevent critical readings from becoming another piece of mastery, a paradox unresolved by most, Cixous writes a text between criticism and fiction that renders the mobility of a *texte-cime* and addresses the reader in an attempt at seduction: "If you read, advance, try to take and let it be known that you too, you are designated to be caught. Your place is reserved in the text, which solicits and cajoles you. . . . Nathanael is speaking to Lothar, but here I am speaking to you; now dance or go away. There must not be a reader in the position of spectator."[11] Cixous's (hollow) writing phallus is itself caught in a structure of doubling, of copies and simulacra. The eye of the law is replaced by a multiplicity of little eyes; everyone is on stage; no one is outside. Reading and writing proceed by *non-savoir*, open but not ignorant. The reader/writer is close to Kleist's puppeteer, who has to feel the center of gravity—or soul—of the puppet and who has to dance himself in order to make the mannequin move *gracefully*.[12] Not the biblical grace but something light, airy, dancing. The writing of fiction is like the image in a concave mirror magnified to its limit, to its disappearance, which suddenly reappears, beyond and upside down. The movement of the puppets—or of fiction—is not that of a straight line with a beginning, middle, and end but that of a curve, a pendulum, or an asymptotic line that brushes against a tangent. The writing of fiction, between artifice and "real," between autonomous doll and authorial hand, always "begins" on the other side or on the side of the other.

A Different Conjugal Logic

Affirming life, reading and writing at the summit, Cixous disrupts the common association of woman with death, so important for dialectics, through her readings of Freud and Hoffmann; Kleist's

Antonia, who will die if her father, Krespel, makes her play the violin; Poe's Morella (*mort elle a:* death she has; *mort est là:* death is here; *more elle a:* the more she has; *elle la mort:* she, death); and of course Joyce, with whom she entertains a long-standing, ambivalent relationship. Admiring Joyce for musicalizing letters and questioning the sign through portmanteau words, Cixous critiques his negative theology, his need to ruse with words in a double gesture, both *capable* and *coupable,* capable and guilty. Joyce accedes to writing, is capable of writing, only after the Fall, with guilt. In the resulting "machine of cruci-fiction," Cixous finds a disquieting eroticism predicated on phallogocentrism and castration, which gradually gives way, from *Exiles* to *Finnegans Wake,* to the writing of a new affective economy. Joyce's erotic structure (read in analytic terms as a belated attachment to the mother) leads to the logical paradox and creative doubt subtending his early works. In a system based on castration, only that which can be enslaved can be possessed. That which is free has to be risked, lost. In this "little" game, the leader chooses a woman on whom another man has "property rights." Desire makes exquisite detours where each person loses and wins. The partners are adversaries, and sexual war is necessary for the desire of recognition to appear. In this (triangular) game, revolving around desire of recognition, one of the people is assigned the role of an object. Love would close the dramatic scene. The logical paradox must be overcome so that woman can approach man in her freedom. This is what is about to happen at the end of "The Dead," where Gabriel reaches the threshold of another space, where his wife could come toward him of her own accord. In order for Gretta to belong to Gabriel as free subject, she must not belong to him. Only Gretta as object, as daughter, whom Gabriel can desire with an animal brutality, can be possessed. The other, the great Gretta, has to be given, risked, lost, to be the one that love may desire. This will not be written until *Finnegans Wake,* where there is no more subject/object division and where desire based on respect of otherness outweighs desire of recognition.[13]

Conjugal scenes in Joyce are most often governed by metaphoric death. There is no real death, but a lesion to be repaired: *la blessure* (the wound), which opens up to sublimation. This logic inscribes in the body strange wounds: mouths, doors, openings from which issue forth works that desire produces to resist the wound or to compensate for it. Loss or gift is ambiguous. Each moment opens onto the moment that annuls or displaces it. This desire, a result of sociocultural circumstances and ideology, must be changed. Cixous reads the possibility for change at the end of Joyce's itinerary in *Finnegans Wake* "on the invisible line separating light from shadow . . . where the limitless 'begins' multiply [in] neither gift nor loss, but a sort of errant grace; and it is only there, but hardly begun in the mixture of singularities, that finally phallocentrism unhooks and blows off course from one to the other border."[14]

About Fictional "Character"

Insisting on the necessity of transforming what she then calls "fiction," Cixous notes that the unified subject has been one with the notion of character. The concept of character, its history and critical presuppositions, are tied to what she, like other new novelists in France, sees as an outmoded literary convention.[15] Character falls in the category of the *déjà là* (the given); hence it is the opposite of the specificity of fiction, which consists in projecting itself into the *non encore là* (the not yet there). Character, from the Greek *khratein*, refers to an engraving, the first mark, the written preserved sign; also to a title, natural or legal, that confers a right, a rank. It is a mark by which the character is assured to be that which has been characterized, and refers to a stamp, an origin. It includes in its lexical evolution that part connected with the art of the portrait, with its distinguishing marks, and is that which morally differentiates one person from the other. Figuratively, it is designed to function more and more as an active element in the process of social coding to the point of becoming an "account," a certificate of conformity, the very mark of intervention of the censor (a detailed report of a person's quality, good repute). Finally, it goes off to appear on the dramatic stage, which is none other than the representation of a real that is not on stage.

Cixous joins French theoreticians of literature in their critique of representation, which they see connected to tradition and conservatism. A text containing character is governed by a coding process that assures its own communicability. Through character, the identification circuit with the reader is established and the commerce between book and reader facilitated. A *community* built on repression consigns its comforts and its goods to this microrelation.[16] Literature thereby assumes value as a marketable form. Mutual leagues and legacies make up a certain literary scene. Cixous situates herself in the mainstream of the French avant-garde writing of the last decade, which frowns on representation as politically reactionary. To break up character and unity, linked to a linear conception of time, is a political gesture necessary to bring about social change. Cixous's project, however, is not just literary and does not simply open a crisis in literature. Her project opens a more general critique (political, social, and moral), and the literary text functions as a privileged locus of expression. She proposes a fiction which by its very definition tears itself away from the *déjà là* and through its "indomitable desire" produces a surplus reality, an excess produced by a subjectivity that has been populated by a mass of egos.[17] A chain forms: woman, writing, poet, excess, (indomitable) desire, gift, surplus of reality. Writing takes place at the level of the imaginary, a Lacanian term Cixous borrows without further elaboration. Making use of Lacan's distinctions between the imaginary and the symbolic, she privileges the former, the realm of identification and doubling. Any relation between two things is necessarily imaginary. Fiction is linked to the imaginary and the Ego as a location of the subject's primary and secondary identifications. As an imaginary nature, the Ego is a function of unawareness that makes ideology and knowledge possible. Hence the importance for those in power to control the production of images, the imaginaries of others. Characterization in fiction is always based on restriction of the imaginary.

The imaginary must be freed through invention of other "I's." The socialization of the subject, its insertion into the social machine, can be obtained only at the expense of controlling the production of the imaginary and the unconscious. These pose threats to the established order that wants to relegate the Ego to its civil place. "Character" and I.D. card go together in this restricting process. Literary interpretation becomes its reinforcement and reflection.

Literary production *and* interpretation are linked to ideology. Against literary production that sustains the status quo, Cixous argues for a new kind of production, a writing from the imaginary, with its infinite multiplicity of identifications precluding a stable subject. She urges for figuration, not characterization, with possibilities of reading in different directions. The new "subject," which as true subject of the unconscious is always on the run, explodes codes and social orders, undoes censorships and repression. It frees, gives birth to writer and reader, breaks the contract, displaces debt and recognition. The author's signature is always multiple.

Writing the Limitless:
Le Troisième Corps, Les Commencements, Neutre

Cixous poetically writes out those strategies in fictional texts. Reading and writing at the confines of Freud, Kleist, Hoffmann, and the rest, and her own biography, she produces fictional theories of theoretical fictions that question genre, work on limits between self and other, masculine and feminine.

In earlier texts, like *Dedans*, Cixous had already written of familial and societal restrictions. *Dedans* had mimed a first *sortie* (a passage out) which was also, paradoxically, a first death. In a phantasmatic representation of her North African childhood, Cixous had written about her position in the family triangle next to her brother, absent (dead) father, and German mother, a practicing midwife who introduced Cixous at an early age to alterity and the guttural sounds of another tongue. Cixous's white sandals of childhood and the hot red Algerian sun contrasted with the mists of northern regions, are motifs which will circulate throughout her texts. *Dedans* poetically weaves an oneiric bloody fabric where the self metamorphoses itself unceasingly.

More theoretical, the three texts published almost simultaneously between 1970 and 1972—*Le Troisième Corps, Les Commencements,* and *Neutre*—anticipate, follow, and comment on each other. *Le Troisième Corps,* seemingly based on representation and lyricism, functions by association rather than by sequence. In dialogue with other texts, it skids from natural catastrophes, earthquakes, volcanic eruptions in Jensen, Freud, and Kleist to earthquake memories from childhood. As accidents break the straight line, the established order with its laws, so do natural catastrophes and war. Volcanic eruptions, earthquakes, battles break the continuity of history and, by analogy, of discourse and law. Earthquakes fissure and crack the transparency of an order just as the unconscious rips apart the apparent homogeneity of logic and meaning.

A female "narrator" writes with her phallus, a hollow phallus whose name is most unstable, T.t (Thod, thot, *tôt*). With echoes from Thoth, the Egyptian god of writing, T.t can be filled with nouns and adjectives, thus subverting the sequence of subject and predicate, as well as the notion of character. The name does not name, it can be read across several languages at once. T.t, the writing phallus of the narrator, doubling her yet never separated from her, her other, not posited as object, circulates throughout the novel. The female narrator writes in effusions and trance where lack is never quite the basis of life.

The opening sentence, "For a long time I closed my eyes when he was leaving,"[18] mocks the opening of *In Search of Lost Time. Le Troisième Corps* does not attempt to recover a lost world but writes an oneiric world without a stable "I," without opposition between presence and absence or distinction between voluntary and involuntary. The written text functions like a dream; the dream is a writing, and the scene of writing mimes the scene of the dream. The logic of the dream, with its nonexclusion of contradiction, functions as a model for the (contradictory) logic of writing, expressing the force of a desire. Yet the dream is not opposed to a waking period, nor is the unconscious opposed to a conscious. The third body, born on the other side of the intersection of the writer's written body and her other, T.t, also undoes repression and functions like an interminable analysis, a *passage* out of a closure.

The female narrator weaves a text of voice, sight, and movement. In phantasmatic scenes of childhood memories and commentaries on Jensen, Freud, and Kleist, Cixous inscribes Bataille's notion of sovereignty and coincidence beyond opposites as elevation and height. For Cixous, close in this to Derrida, couples of opposites such as masculine and feminine take off from a residue (*fond*) of diacritical and differing reserve. Already differing, this reserve, which "precedes" the opposition of differing effects, does not have the punctual simplicity of a *coincidentia oppositorum*.[19] Whereas in Derrida excess as that which cannot be recuperated in a "system," into conceptual oppositions, is not necessarily on the side of abundance, Cixous, closer to Bataille, writes of excess as effusion, eros, poetry, drunkenness, and laughter. Derrida, reading Hegel via Bataille, notes that laughter exceeds dialectics and negativity but never appears. It exceeds the very possibility of meaning. In the dialectical system, poetry, laughter, and ecstasy are nothing. The Hegelian notion of sublation is laughable in that it signifies the busying of a discourse losing its breath (*s'essoufflant*), trying to reappropriate all negativity for itself as it works risking into an investment, as it amortizes absolute spending and gives meaning to death, blinding itself to the bottomlessness of nonmeaning from which meaning is drawn.[20] Exceeding Derrida's philosophical meditations, Cixous inscribes effusion and laughter through poetic effects which, in the wake of Bataille, open the space of the sacred. Meaning (the meaning of nonmeaning) has always been linked to discursive signification. But meaningful discourse is not opposed to the sacred poetic word. The poetic is that which in every discourse can open up to the absolute loss of meaning, to the bottomlessness of the sacred, of nonmeaning, of play, to the loss of consciousness from which it awakens with a throw of the dice. Not an absence of meaning, which would once again subordinate poetry to discourse, but a nonmeaning in meaning, an affirmation of sovereignty.[21] The temporal mode of this writing is the instant, not the point of full presence, the instant that slides and eludes between two presences, difference as elusive affirmation of presence.

In Jensen's *Gradiva*, Hanold Norbert is in love with Zoe Bertgang, the girl from next door. He represses his love and adores instead Gradiva, the reproduction of a girl from a Roman bas-relief whom he believes to have been buried in the cataclysm of Pompeii (yet another form of repression). The sequence is inverted; Hanold is in love with an image. It is Gradiva, the father's daughter—there is no mention of a mother—who helps Hanold, during a trip to Pompeii, to declare his love. During his search, Hanold watches Gradiva disappear and reappear like a lizard between the columns.

Cixous writes a text from those fissures—in French a play on *lizard* (lizard) and *lézarde* (fissure)—between conscious and unconscious, a text of *sortie*, crisscrossed by the fulgurating *z*'s. The real name of Gradiva (the one who advances) is Zoe (life), whose absent letter is reinscribed throughout the text as Zoe *Bert*gang (walk, the step) intersects with Nor*bert* from the misty north. A text of limits, between north and south, masculine and feminine, dream (hallucination) and consciousness, it advances gracefully in dancing steps of *sortie*. In Jensen's text, Zoe is the one who brings to life Norbert's repressed love in a kind of feminine transfer that Freud never mentioned. Cixous uses Freud's discoveries of unconscious and dream but turns her back on him in parricidal fashion to write her own and Gradiva's way out. Sexual difference must be reinscribed beyond the simple possibility of reversals. Everything in Cixous's text is double. The female narrator dialogues with her masculine components and with other readings. Nothing refers to a simple origin.

Taking off from Gradiva's step, she and her other stage their own excessive scene. In the bas-relief, Gradiva's frozen gait simulates a vertical dancing movement of *sortie* linked to verticality. Gradiva, real or statue, immobile in her movement, soars in splendor like some of her later avatars, Cixous's Penthesilea and Cleopatra. The airy, ascending text writes the winged ease (*l'aisance ailée*) of Gradiva, whose feet clad in light sandals barely touch the ground. The white sandals of Cixous's own Algerian childhood, metamorphosed into those of Gradiva, function as an artificial lure that propels the text in dancing steps of explosive *sorties*. The gait of the Gradiva and that of the narrator mime the movement of writing, immobile in its immobility. They stage the Lacanian pronouncement on the fading of the subject—always about to disappear. The writing never posits itself, never becomes discourse or object to be analyzed. The movement is one of verticality and gracefulness as in these two scenes rewritten by Cixous from Jensen:

> The left foot set ahead and the right preparing to follow only touches the ground with the tip of the toes, while the sole and heel rise up almost vertically. This movement of a disappearance which is on the verge of disappearing seduces us.[22]

> The dress which the Gradiva wore on the day of the eruption covered her almost to her ankles, but the large number of folds which filled her below the belt gave to what could have been a thick girdle hindering her gait an extraordinary suppleness. She wore sandals.[23]

Following a well-known poetic paradox, Cixous suggests that since total disappearance would be nothingness, reversible in yet another system of totality, the text must mime a movement about to disappear. Just as the light-footed Gradiva, her dress with countless folds flowing about her, barely touches the ground, Cixous's narrative, leaping from one text to another, never stops or congeals meanings. The text is double; it performs rhythmically its dancing steps and writes about those movements. It never becomes a representation with an outside reality. *Tout s'abîme* into copy of copy and simulacra.

After reflecting that she and T.t have a similar gait, *je* adds: "The way we mime elevation, flight, does not deceive; those who practice it seek each other out right away. They guess from the vertical foot position toward what happy regions you are bound."[24] Flight and height, metaphors common to Nietzsche and Bataille, make the text spin in a space beyond the coincidence of inside and outside, conscious and unconscious, possible and impossible, where temporal succession has not been introduced yet.

Questions rather than answers, no frontal attacks. Parricidal writing questions the law of the father. It does not lead back to an origin; one is always already written, and repetition is originary. The writing is one of scenes, always double, where sameness is traversed by otherness, life by death, masculine by feminine. Concepts are written and effaced. Derrida had written in *Voice and Phenomenon,* "an indefinite skidding of signs as erring and changing of scenes (*Verwandlung*) linking one re-presentation to the next without beginning or end."[25] There is no more representation of a real, no beginning or end, no eye of the law that sees from the outside. The glass through which a "real"—always coded by ideology—is filtered must be shattered. Writing does not represent a "real" but phantasmatically stages and poetically shatters concepts and meaning:

I leaned against the glass door at its neuralgic point so that it broke suddenly with an unknown noise of thunder, harsh screams of the glass, breaking of vertebrae, horrible shattering of an almost human body, explosion of meaning, which destroy the myth of the traced way, for one will be able from now on to go from the center through all the other meanings in all directions, points of truth which are staked in all corners, even the most remote of my memory and of my eyes. Fulgurations which do not leave any quarters, all is taken in a light which surprises furtivities, the most banal scenes are torn by scenes of unheard violence; finished are ceremonies, prudences, concessions; the curtains burn, burnt eyelashes fall from my eyelids into the hollow of my neck, blood flows in Pompeii, flows into dried-up beds and dead veins. Pompeii rises, I am Caesar traversed from all sides, I am in bliss and enjoy without pain my twenty flows. But says my reasonable memory: Caesar is not a woman, is not you: it is useless here in the powerful light of our eyes, there is no limit, Caesar helps me to pour my blood which is red. What is without limits?[26]

Curtains, screens of memory, everything burns in an immense holocaust. Writing becomes bliss, it speaks that *jouissance* which had been silenced. Laws of society, all that shelters, curtains, eyelashes, all that veils is burnt in a violent cataclysm or catastrophe exploding limits, undoing oppositions between genders, proper and figurative meaning. Gone are the poetic myths relegating woman to death; gone are the sirens of yesteryear who sing at a distance: "A detail, a window in my room in the strange house with the glass door opens up on an elevated garden cemetery. I am told that under the stones the bodies of the drowned of love are resting, they are sirens, they have soft accusations against men inscribed in convex stones."[27]

To these funerary inscriptions and songs of woes on phallic tombstones, these testaments, Cixous opposes a new song, a limitless, blissfull writing which in effusion spills over all boundaries. From vertiginous heights the narrator calls her lover, her other: "Yes, I see it all, I see the light that flows from my eyelids, I bathe all the bodies, those who have lived and those who live. I am tormented by my own power with giant laughter. Carry the world with me, my love who has carried me in your flesh when I did not see anything anymore."[28] The affirmative, artistic narrator, drunk with absolute power, who through her explosive laughter feels the bliss of existence in an instant, calls her other, her lover, her reader from whom she is never separated. Self and other give birth to each other; kinship roles are endlessly substitutable. Gone is the allegory of a family romance.

Beyond separation, one is always inscribed in the other, without origin: "No first couple, no engendering pair. Only daughter and virgin to be done over again. At all moments I want to be able to go back into that body, that thought, at any moment to be able to be in front of him, as in front of the wall of the temple which does not exist, which exists only if I am the door and if I am the wall. I cannot do without your body, completely other and from which I have not first exited."[29] The play of masculine, feminine, same, and other intersect at the textual level: "Same and other meet at the crossing of our languages, a third body happened to us, where there is no law."[30] Reading at this limit, the inscriber intersects with the inscribed, there where separation separates from itself, where the critical text is not separated from the primary text which it controls. Separation is no longer identical to itself, reversible into its opposite; it is traversed by its own difference. The female reader/writer is the limit and the transgression of that limit. "She is the skin of the dream and dreams that skin."[31] Her eye is not that of the law but the pupil (*pupille*), which sees itself see from all sides. Her active affirmation is also an attitude of extreme passivity: "I let things be done to me by whoever materializes me until one can no longer distinguish masculine from feminine. To the letter, here He is She. She is He. He or she is the marrow and the blood of the beauty (of hers, of his). There are ravishing moments when we no longer know which one of us is the mother, which one is God."[32] Power, exuberance, height, affirmation form the chain subtending this writing. They are all in a position of excess, less here through textual play or syntactic operations than through sheer abundance of transgressive affirmations. In this climate of exuberance, sexual opposites coincide without fusion, *masculin e(s)t féminin, féminin e(s)t masculin*. The female writer does not repress her masculine sexual components but writes from where one continuously defers the other. Kinship structures are not to be thought outside any linguistic configurations.[33] Maternal effects are not necessarily tied to the body of the person thus designated by a cultural role.

Echoing Blake's aphorism, which Bataille used as epigraph for *La Part maudite*, Cixous writes: "Exuberance is beautiful." The beautiful is excess; it is that which is not functional, utilitarian, pragmatic, reasonable, which tears apart and can kill. It is on the side of pure spending. Hence Cixous's attraction to the fiction of Kleist, a constant in all of her writings. In his *Earthquake in Chile*, the transgressive lovers Jeronimo and Josepha, condemned by society and about to be executed, are rescued by an act of God, an earthquake that cracks prison walls and upsets human order. Their reprieve is of short duration, and they pay for their love with death in a society unable to tolerate any kind of grace. Similarly, *The Marquise von O* stages the triumph of love and innocence. The zigzagging writing, intense like lightning, produces a feverish, oneiric text in which Count F., a letter without a name, ubiquitous and unseizable, in a constant state of metamorphosis, moves the threads of the text. His power is immediate, absolute. For Cixous, the letter *F* (fire, phallus, friction, fiction, etc.) leaves in the other's bosom (*sein*) "a mark of that writing which does not have to repeat itself to be heard."[34] This silent, corporeal writing is far from that secondary writing considered to be a transcription of speech. MetaFor is no longer a trope substituting for a proper, but all language is necessarily metaphoric, in movement more than a transport from one post to another.

Texts of beginnings, yet in which the beginning always follows, and where as in *Les Commencements* the oneiric fabric is woven from a state of sovereign indifference, outside limits, all that divides, compartmentalizes:

I was in the dream and the dream was in my will. I was preoccupied by the locus where I was dreaming. There, I was for the first time of an innocence which did not know itself, which did not know me any longer and which could not be seen and which was this inconceivable and real margin where I could be in the dream while it was within me, where I was not bothered by having my entrails for skin. This innocence had no common or proper noun. It is only the name which I had to qualify later on, in order to talk to Saint George, the condition of sovereign indifference which would read me there where everything is possible because succession has not been introduced yet.[35]

In this non-locus of dream where all is possible, where language knows no contradiction, one is of a true innocence, an innocence not reversible into guilt.

In *Les Commencements,* literary scenes are replaced by paintings (framed representations). Titian's Saint George, both angel (eagle) and dragon, steps out of the frame and represents his own representation. *Aile et plume* (wing and feather/pen), *uccello* (bird) and by paronomasia *ocelle* (little eye of the text)—the text moves by skidding and splitting. Saint George has certain realistic traits, but again his name is subjected to various decompositions by the narrator: *sein et gorge* (breast, being, and throat—that is, the seat of voice), *sang* (blood), *geint* (bemoaned), *singe* (monkey). The legendary male hero becomes his own double. He sees when the scale falls from his eye at the same time that the scale reflects him. All is caught in a web of differences. The subject is born of that signifier that comes from the other, is momentarily petrified into a signifier but, as true subject of the unconscious and always on the run, immediately goes on to another signifier. The subject as effect of the signifier exists only in relation to other signifiers.[36]

In a reenactment of the Freudian *fort/da,* in a scene of intense desire, the narrator, in stride, intersects with Saint George. The scene is witnessed by the prophetic eye which, far from the eye of the law, is that little eye on the foot of the narrator and which, opening onto movement, walk, and metaphor, is one of *sortie.* The eye is a left—that is, false—amimetic eye of Judas. It opens onto a writing in which reflection and mimesis are originary.

Saint George closed his eyes each time I arrived in front of him with suffering and fear and softness. Walk! I pivoted, I walked, I saw him look at me through my back, and I was looking at him while I was advancing toward the crossing in the shape of X with my eye of Essor. At the ninth coming and going, he gets up, holds me back. He has superb immobility, which figures the desire to die of love, and if I close all my eyes, it is to lose myself. Da. Take, take, take. Fort. Disappear the self.[37]

The eye of Essor, that hieroglyphic eye replacing the law, reads as *essor* (jump), *et sort* (and goes out), *des sorts* (of destinies, of chance). The scene is similar to that in *Le Troisième Corps.* Selves are shed (*dépassés*) in a violent explosion of love at the crossings of desires that may kill.

If the scene is in the shadow of the father, the mother is never quite absent. In *Les Commencements,* it is the arrival of the mother Eve that makes the event (*évé-ne-ment,* the event and the mother who speaks the truth). The passage of Eve, of the mother, invites a return to a different origin, a different source of appeasement and love. In Nietzschean fashion, Cixous displaces the old phallocentric architectural metaphor of woman-as-house. She suggests the proximity of the mother-as-house but without doors, with open arches overlooking the sea. From the mother's terrace, a look at the sea undoes established laws of syntax: eyes do not penetrate but touch eminently caressive, supple waters, and their look does not leave a trace. These absolutely transparent waters, without shadow, therefore independent of natural light, have their own luminous source. The narrator asks: "Where is the man, where is the child who would not fear in trembling the absolute simplicity of a mother, who would not fear the supple mother, without resistance, all red waters, lit, thick, red liquid, creamy, and still immaterial, since neither the color, nor the surface, nor the depth can be disturbed by a missile?"[38]

The reaction one feels toward the mother, contrary to that which one feels toward the lover, is one of absolute vertigo that comes from the heart, not from intelligence with its machinations of possible and impossible. If a questioning of paternal authority, a dividing of the origin, results in transforming *le commencement* into *les commencements* in such a way that the beginning always follows, the mother *is: sans commencement* (without beginning). And Cixous makes the following qualitative portrait of the mother:

> Eve never lies.
> My mother is where she is.
> She is not where she is not.
> Eve never lies.[39]

The calm portrait of the mother anticipates something that stirs underneath the paternal violence and that moves toward the feminine question, but first, Cixous further generalizes her practice of grafting.

In *Neutre,* a "textual opera," all is happening at the limits of earth and sea where a crowd of phantasms, masks, doubles, quotes from poets and revolutionaries enter and exit: Marx, Freud, Shakespeare but also Dante, Hölderlin, Milton, Poe. *Neutre,* ne-uter, neither one (sex) nor the other, is a *ré-cit du récit,* a narrative of narrative or quotation of quotation, an errant writing without simple origin where doubles proliferate. In *Neutre,* the possibility of narrative (in French, *histoire,* with its double meaning of story and history) is questioned through a practice of *greffe* (grafting) of words and sounds from other texts. The sixth side of the die is nothing but an effect. "Thus the thing [*la chose*] writes itself,"[40] according to the chance of a dice roll. *La chose* is not hidden to be revealed; it is but an effect of surface, of grafting.

The text does not have a simple beginning. Its various epigrams relate it to other texts and other disciplines. A holocaust burns all signs and identities. "If without name, without strength, without age, and without seeing, I am."[41] Without light, space, and time, all predicates of being, but with movement and desire. Parts are severed from the body which, no longer whole and identical to itself, neither castrating nor castrated, neither one sex nor the other, continually engenders itself. Everything is double; the text quotes itself: "One is not without the other, 'one is not without the other,' "[42] nor f without f' nor J without J' nor masculine without feminine. The reader, via Shakespeare's *Hamlet,* is invited to listen to her false twin, to phantom sounds.

In this delirious procession, words are bent backwards at an angle, myths and their allegorical messages exploded, castration mocked through a rewriting of the mythological couple Samson and Delilah. Samson's name, guaranteeing his strength and masculinity, is subjected to treacherous treatment by Delilah, who—paradoxically—binds while she unbinds. She effracts Samson's identity as his noun is cut into: *sans, sans:* dividing himself from himself; *sans sang:*

without blood, the bloodless cut; *sans son;* without sound, without voice but with phantom sounds; *son son: cent sangs, cent cent* (sound sound, a hundred bloods, a hundred hundred). Through the ruse of Delilah's writing, the mythological figure and its exemplary truth fall into an abyss of his own name which unnames. *Neutre* is a bloody text, *sanglant* and *sans gland,* without genealogy or tree but one in which each graft, each cut, leads to another graft. Samson and Delilah do not embody an allegorical truth, law, and hierarchy. Through divisibility of the name, a first allegory is exploded.

Neutre introduces a coin into the archives of academic literary criticism and its ideology. Neither fiction nor criticism, it is an impersonal, secret narration cutting between institutionalized barriers. It consists of "métaphores mal jointes" in semantic random, in a dice roll. The letter *sème* and *s'aime:* it sows and likes itself. Cixous's operation of grafting consists in "plugging in at random the greatest number of parts possible." No head, no beginning: "To make parts of one's own body, to give them sometimes a human figure, rarely a tropological figure, to draw new and uncalculated riches from this virtual marriage."[43] The narrative *file,* it flees and weaves, does not posit itself, does not land. A hieroglyphic writing where the letter *fait air (R) ou aile (L),* it makes air/er/he or wing/*elle*/she at the same time as it errs and wanders (*erre*).

The subject as textual machine writes and is written; the autobiographical "narrative" functions like an analysis. *Neutre* writes the letter before the law, f (*feu,* fiction, *fil, fils;* and by phonic contiguity, phallus, phoenix, etc.) in a writing that is both written and erased. The reader is invited to read the other text, which flows where the first one burns. This *ré-cit à vide* undoes traditional rhetoric. Since nothing is metaphor, all is metaphor; allegory with its laws, subtext, and subnarrative is exploded into sparks and wings (*ailes*) and prelinguistic figures. There is no possible reduction to a truth or oedipal scenario. This narration of narration is also the history of the subject: "There is mouth but not yet word, there is son but not yet name, there is desire but not yet sex."[44] *Neutre,* under the sign of the phoenix, is written from this non-locus of sexual indecision in a language that burns and is born from the ashes. Desire confronts death, which does not yet, as in subsequent writings, wear the mask of the masculine.

Writing and the Law: Portrait du soleil

Each subject is born, comes onto herself from the other in an endless play of substitutions and identifications linked to passage in time, like the sun or that other signifier beginning with a sinewy S (the very S of that barred Subject), Sand—with echoes from Hoffmann's *Sandman*—the grains of which are so innumerable and the mobility so great that she who digs does not know whether the sand digs her. To write the (infinite) story of the subject is as impossible as to make the portrait of the sun or to count the grains of sand.

From Bataille, "*La Differance*," *Les Ecrits,* Freud, Rembrandt's portraits—those points of juncture in the network of the dream—the orange flowers of the narrator, Dora's white flowers, Cixous writes a fulgurating, decapitating text. The word *décollement* refers at the same time to a beheading and the taking off of a plane, a textual machine replacing an individual control of language. A parricidal writing, sinewy like the S and slashing like the aggressively hissing Z that, by phonic omission, conjoins the paternal Vienna to the amorous Venize.

At the confines of "*La Differance*" and "*Subversion du sujet et dialectique du désir dans l'inconscient freudien,*" the relation to the other is one of desire and love-as-passion, beyond a simple dichotomy of *tueur-tué* (killer and victim), in a network of power relations that shift back and forth, always in time, the way the sand flows in the hourglass, in an endless movement of reversals. The devices are similar to those in other novels. The narrator lies in bed at night, between sleep and dream; she writes with her ubiquitous phallus Jeor, a rest from Saint George, *Je or, jeu or,* play and gold, a most unstable other always about to disappear, whose phonemes circulate throughout the text in a general economy contrasted to the limited circulation of the family machine in Freud's *Dora*.

Portrait du soleil is an overtly autobiographical text whose title mockingly carries echoes of Western heliocentrism. The sun is the origin, father, god, and capital. To make the portrait of the sun is to represent that which cannot be looked at, like death, to defy it, to make the impossible possible, to represent the impossible, to double that which is unique, to make it a proliferation of copies. To look at the sun is blinding and evokes castration. *Portrait* in a certain way is a feminine story of the eye, not one that beholds its object at a distance in a reappropriating manner but one that reinscribes the structure of the eye differentially. In a mixture of oneiric and erotic scenes, Cixous, beholding her male friend stretched out at her side, monologues in dialogue. Lyricism and expression drift again into a web of intertextuality, beyond genres, defying the notion of creator, author, originality, one with property and authority. The narrator in flight and theft (*en vol*) writes, steals, quotes without diacritical marks signaling the debt. *Portrait* becomes that third body born beyond the intersection of reading and writing.

Yet *Portrait* is not a biography of fact and description. The "subject" as subject of the unconscious is always born from the other and is always about to disappear. It never constitutes itself as a subject that can be identified. Words and phonemes exist only in relation to other words, other phonemes. Cixous opts for a corporeal writing before a division of body and mind, a purifying writing signed with her blood: "*Et maintenant de quel sang signer ça?*" (And now, with what blood sign this?) reads the last line.[45] This is not just a cheap tongue twister of the kind all French children are subjected to in grammar class but a putting into question of the authorship of the text. *Sang*, blood and *sans*, without, in and out; *s(a)igner*: to bleed and to sign, *ça*: it/id, *sa* (signifier) from Saussure or Hegel's SA (*savoir absolu*, absolute knowledge). It becomes the authorless signature of a writing before the law, before separation where the *nom propre* is *non propre*. This writing in which letters in lower case circulate freely in the bloodstream undoes personal and collective repressions through dreams, poetry, demystification of the oedipal myth with its connotations of incest, separation from the mother, and constitution of the "opposite" sex. Chronology, its unfolding in history, gives way to the phantasm with its own temporality. The phantasm, wearing the mask of death, must be pushed back.

The tone, in the opening pages, is bloody and aggressive: "One must choose a blood orange. At night, blood goes back in time. Every living being has blood that comes back at night. To ease the return, I eat my blood orange."[46] Dream, where temporal succession has not yet been introduced, facilitates a re-traversal of the origin. Letters circulate as the timeless blood surges and the bloody juices of the orange flow through the narrator's veins. Orange becomes the simulacrum of the hot red sun, a sun no longer distant and unattainable but a color, a quotidian fruit, a lure that opens the narrative and proliferates in the text, an orange that opens the flow of blood and is also the origin of the narrator. The sun-orange-origin: *Oran-je*, Oran-I, from Oran am I. Oran, Cixous's native city, is metamorphosed into the orange. A non-origin, the capital letter is replaced by a letter in lower case, the uniqueness by a proliferation of fruity simulacra. A first separation, a first cut, is but a first disjunction: a word cut and grafted onto other words. "The first time I cut a word, it was it [the orange]."[47] The narrator cuts the fruit into uneven halves to avoid symmetry. "I will traverse the *oranje*, I will go and sit on the knees of Jeor, and I will put my arms around his neck; the sky around our bodies will be of that phosphorescent blue which flows into his glass vase in the absence of the sun. To Jeor I will tell the worst [a play on *père/pire*, father/worst], and he will tell me who I am."[48] (Parricidal) traversal of the origin leads Cixous to write with her phallus legitimized by her good father's refracting blue eyes. Though mocking the phallus, the writer is still in a masculine structure.

The date: *le dix fièvrier 1970. Dix, dis:* ten and say; f(i)èvrier: February and fever. A feverish writing of trance, an upsurge of life, an effusion into writing of all life lifting up a writing in fusion. *Jeudi, jeu dit:* Thursday and a game said, affirmed. *Je(u):* I as play. The body of the narrator, feverish and playful, peels and eats the orange and is eaten by it. This nondialectical simultaneity of eating and being eaten prevents the reversal inherent in a traditional concept of violence in which the killer becomes the victim, identifies with her, and stops violence. Real "sovereign" violence, exclaims Cixous, is not re-cuperable by dialectics or by hierarchies. "*L'éventrement de la sol-eille,*" the ripping of the she-sun, is the true, impossible violence that forever rips and diffuses the text.

Cixous's North African origin, with its blood—"ancient, well known, too salty, unappeasable, overheated"[49]—and the Egyptian hieroglyph, is contrasted with her northern origin. She and Jeor are in a place called Masterdam, an obvious anagram of Amsterdam, with its portraits by Rembrandt and reminiscences of Freud and psychoanalytic concepts: "*un jeudit enfiévré de Masterdam,*"[50] a feverish Thursday/spoken game of Masterdam. What happens when the master becomes mad, when fever shakes the master and all is a game with rules but no (linear) directions, where no reassur-ing order assigns each subject its place but where anguish and exhil-aration comes from infinite substitutability? Writing becomes ethe-real, light, in flight, not directed by the sun. Free circulation is supported on the semantic level by verbal activity. Verbs of flight, "to push, to search, to ascend, and to fever are the verbs that carry me off."[51] The subject as textual machine is kept moving by props like cars, airplanes, and other vehicles, transporting the narrator's writing and desire.

Verbs of liquefaction also diffuse the writing: "There is the tor-ment of torment, where one sees blood traverse the eyelids of mem-ory dripping with the past. . . . Blood traverses, ascends, spreads, constellates, prophesizes, ironizes, even appears orange, belies my eyes which see Dieubis in black, which want to see black, but the blood flows back into my eyes in the middle of the night, in a way which cannot be negated, shining orange, trace of what could have been, proof of that which is being able to be."[52] The scene is one of inner sight, dream eyes, of the body seen and felt with eyes closed. A sight that does not distance, appropriate, take pleasure in seeing the debt one feels, that reduces distance, temporal and spatial. A sight without separation. Oneiric temporality with all its shortcuts, distortions, and jumps replaces linear time linked to a false concept of consciousness and unity. Opposites "coincide" but always over an already differing reserve, where red and black become orange or *Oran-je.*

Scenes flow in rapid succession, never quite present, separated, but always half-born shapes, emerging from a liquid element in a continuous birth asserting itself over death. "A prey of all tenses through this blood, I am a prey of all senses [in French, all meanings and all senses]. What flows has already traversed me, blood and milk, urine and tears. I flow, I am being flown [or molded] without ever dying."[53] The space of the kitchen, the traditional social space of the woman, takes on cosmic dimensions and brings writing, which preserves, as close as possible to something that can be tasted and consumed. Cixous writes: "I am putting together things in order to see the effect: a cosmic kitchen with raw stars . . . a series of furiously adored objects . . . a series of celluloid bathers hesitating on the nature of their sex; an unknown, my letters, some horseradish [*meerrettich*]."[54] Stellar writing brings down the laws from the sky into the kitchen. Hierarchies collapse. The writer, like the puppeteer, assembles her objects, neither inanimate nor animate, neither masculine nor feminine. The German word *meerrettich,* in lower case, irrupts into the French text, preventing it from closing upon itself. The vegetable, outside of any genealogy, diffuses its multiplicity of doubles, *ee, rr, tt,* carrying echoes from the seamother (*mer-mère*), more (*mehr*), to salvage (*retten*), I (*ich*), or you (*tich, dich*). Letters before the law, before symbolization, proliferate and move like sand, another double of the sun. F, M, X, K, Z. F, Freud, *flic* (policeman); M, the median letter, same and other, the mobile bar; X, a barred chiasm as in Cixous; K from Kafka's parable of the law or Mr. K. in *Dora;* Z, not a slash but a reversible letter of intensity and lightning which conjoins places and people: *Vienne* and *Venise* (Vienna and

Venice). Cixous listens to an inner rhythm. Her work on language is less a play on signifiers than a phantasmatic rewriting of a "real." Psychoanalytic concepts are written out in a mixture of the horrible and the sublime, without respect for decorum.

Portrait is also a rewriting of the Dora case. Freud, who wrote about Dora in the latter's absence, is himself on stage. Portrait of the sun, of the golden Dora's adored father, of Mr. K., Father Freud, the narrator's father, her lovers. A story of fathers where the mother is only briefly mentioned, in the museum of Dresden, during Dora's contemplation of the Madonna—*portrait de Dora*—whose motherly gestures she so admires.

Critical of Dora's "vulgar sexuality" and far from glorifying the hysteric, whom she will follow through *La Jeune Née, LA,* and the play *Portrait de Dora,* Cixous admires her courageous "no" that jams the smooth functioning of the social and family machine. At the limit self-defeating, since it ebbs back into silence, Dora's gesture was the only one possible at a certain historical moment, in a certain cultural configuration. Cixous mocks the limited circulation of the family machine, governed by a symbolic order and the name of the father: "Papa-Mama-Dora-Mr K-Mrs K-Papa-Mrs K-Dora-Mr K-Dora-Papa-Mrs K-Mama-Papa-Dora-My treasure-My pearl-My jewel-Papa-Dora-My little jewel-Mrs K-Jeor-Mrs F-Dora-God-bis."[55]

Dora's unspoken desire for Mrs. K. and Mr. K., as well as for her father, her attractions to masculine *and* feminine, raise the question of a "feminine desire" and of the closure of genre. "I have already thought of that possibility; on several occasions I have tried to cross the line of genders."[56] So notes Cixous, anticipating a bisexual (missexual) writing of difference. In Cixous's text, Freud no longer pulls the strings; he becomes an actor on stage himself. *Portrait* rewrites part of the Dora case from a feminine angle. Dora is born from a *sortie,* a departure from the masculine structure, away from Mr. K., out of her transfer onto Freud.

Gradiva's step—"and pulling up lightly her dress with her left hand, Gradiva Rediviva, Zoe Bertgang, surrounded by Hanold's dreamy looks, with her supple and calm gait, in the full sun, on the stones, stepped across the street"[57]—is metamorphosed into that of Dora both in *Portrait du soleil* and the later play, *Portrait de Dora.* Cixous rewrites Dora to the tune of Gradiva:

> It was the most *hors-eux* [happy and outside of them] day of her life. She crossed the street dryfooted, lifting her dress with the tips of her fingers in a gesture that barely uncovered her ankles. The inside of Mr. K. was hell, his outside was still becoming. He had seen Dora pass by. There is no greater pain than to remember happy days in the midst of misery, and that Freud knew. If he had not been a doctor, he would have fallen like a poet; Freud too was a tender father.[58]

Gradiva-Dora's step breaks down the smooth circulation of women around men, including Cixous's own around her analytic father Freud.

The Letter in Lower Case: Partie

Crucial to a rewriting of the play between masculine and feminine is the status of the letter that allows one to focus on the other. In *Portrait,* the circulation of letters—F, M, X, K, Z—is very important but not so much as in another piece of the same period, *Partie,* one of the most neo-Joycean works in France to date and one of Cixous's most experimental. A virile *Plus-je,* who is always more than one, more "I" or eye, advances toward an inverted *Si-je,* unseizable and divisible, in a mockery of a Homeric epic. The overdetermination of portmanteau words questions Western logocentrism, with its division between body and spirit. The text solicits the eye as much as the ear. In *Partie,* the part always exceeds the whole, defies any totalization. As we have seen in *Portrait,* the status of the letter is crucial for our reading of Cixous's texts. Numerous are the essays that provide a background to Cixous's poetics. Simply put, after Freud's distinction of a primary and a secondary process, a mark or impression of the alphabet is a symbolic shifter that allows one to discourse or to focus on the other. As an "instance," the point or form situates a barred chiasm by which the ratiocinating subject can behold the energy of its constitution but always with the effect of frustration, to the degree that the letter has been lost since the thinking—or acculturated—person has entered into society with its generally oedipal mechanics. The letter—whether an A, M, K, X, or Z—can be said to remind the subject at privileged moments of regressive cognition of a preconstrictive time when questions of paternity, incest, or the opposition between body and mind, masculine and feminine, did not exist.[59] In its figural shape, not representing anything other than itself, the letter in lower case promises both accession to the world and its contrary, both liberation and frustration. As such, its (obsessive) inscription in the pagelike psyche allows the analyst to suture the manifest expression of the patient to the latent situation enveloped about it. Cixous maintains the letter in an immanent bind of cognition, body, and world. She uses the conclusions of Lacan's readings of Freud to make of the flow of *belles lettres* an amniotic current by which reader and writer, unified, force a synaesthesia of language and world, of letter and music. In a sense, Cixous returns here and now to that idealized area which has been barred for others by the letter. She does so via the imagination, which is to say via the drive to make writing not the gloss on but an unending identity of the world, where lack is not completely the basis of life.

The problematic is best situated in her rewriting of Joyce. Where certain sequences of *Ulysses* and *Finnegans Wake* epiphanize the reader/writer so that the body may be unmoored from contingency in a conflation and dispersion of meaningful language—or history—she notes how the visibility of the printed page will finally be in harmonic cadence with the music that has had a tendency to make the letter disappear. In her fiction, these areas are put forward to change our dulled senses, and they have their greatest effect in the concern with the immediacy of the woman's cause in contemporary France.

The model of Joyce's prosody allows her to break dialectics and the authority of Hegel in his own "name." In *Partie*, the patrimony of letters, arts, and sciences is figured by Hegueule, homonymic with Hegel, in dialogue with the "central" character, Plusje. The story concerns the coming into being of the latter, whose voice, which had been the stuff of myth and false paternity, finally accedes to visibility:

> The alter-echo apostrophizes rudely:
> Hegueule: The fathermore goes out of him-
> self in the other to come back to himself.
>
> Plusje: Every auffher must take off in its
> offher . . .
>
> A nounson bears not
>
> A nounson be-ears of his own desires
>
> Hegueule: Forself of one depends on the forself of the offher.
>
> Readhor: and how many states runs Plus-je?
>
> Plusje: me I layover always surplus of nine
> my nine
>
> Hegueule: Thusleave a norfathernorson[60]

The Hegelian dialectic of master and slave, father and son, or state and family is stuffed back into the mouth of the narrator whose voice must talk on the printed page. Hence a parallelism derived from the characters seizing two phonic shapes at once and, in their seizure, a multiplication of meanings destroying the limits that melano- or phonocentric adepts—Homer and Hegel—prescribed for the listening world. *Homère* becomes *Ohmère,* an apostrophe to the mother (*Oh mère*) whose opening loins give birth to voice through writing; and *Hegueule,* as I have suggested, makes for "He-gueule," or "Him-shout/snout" who had aligned the spiritual with the "masculine instance" of invisibility. That phallocentric privilege of the male who can turn the other into images without himself being typed or photographed is what Cixous's misspelling breaks apart. The traditional one-sidedness of representation is put in question in such a way that the female—the person who can apostrophize the mother—can accede to writing which is one with endless birth.

It remains for us to situate better the Hegelian instance Cixous undoes. In a study of the problematic position of writing in the philosopher's project, Jacques Derrida, whose logical investigations Cixous's fiction often exceeds, determined how all of Hegel's philosophy depends on an impossible deferment of writing; in the evolution of the spirit from East to West, the ideogram must cede to phonic writing. In this scheme the funerary inscription of hieroglyphics on steles commemorating death is to give way to a writing that must become transparent and even disappear in favor of breath and *Geist*. Writing impedes—but also originates—the evolution of the mind. The more Hegel wants to leave writing, the more he goes back to it, the more its visible presence gives reason—and death— to his system. Derrida's reading in fact crowns an argument for a "simultaneous priority" of writing, a *pro-gramme* (a letter put forward) that will problematize all the contradictions of voice and script in major philosophical texts of the Occidental tradition. Although this was announced only briefly in 1967, Derrida's case for the letter has been carried out with obsessive rigor paralleled only by the production of Cixous. Following Cixous's *Partie* with identical intent and effect, he opens *Glas* with a neo-Saussurean reading of the proper name in order to make the signless signature a fragment of an impossible graft of letter and sound, an eagle whose place in the sun incites the reader to blind herself in looking for its shape, and a mirror whose sight effaces the presence of the subject Hegel had willed to maintain: ET GEL, EST GEL, E GEL, HE GL, and the impronounceable . . . ; even a crystalline block of ice identical in difference to the sun of which it is a part.

> His name is so strange. Of the eagle he
> holds imperial or historical power. Those
> who pronounce him still with a French

accent, there are some, are ridiculous to a
certain point: the semantically infallible
restitution, for the one who has read him a
little, only a little, of the magistral coldness
and of the imperturbable seriousness, the
eagle taken in ice and jell.

Be thus frozen the emblemished philosopher.[61]

Where Derrida puts him between nadir and zenith, Cixous had
placed him in the master's mouth. That "impossible" position of the
name that can be neither eaten nor rendered is precisely that of the
letter reimagined and rematerialized from the conceptual status it
had acquired in neo-Freudian psychoanalysis.

In returning to the fragment of *Partie* above, we begin to see how
Cixous immobilizes Derrida's case for letters in coordination with a
femin*ist* cause. For Hegel, movement of life begins in a separation
that the male always recuperates for his own ends: the father produces the son in a dialectic with the female so that the child will fit
in a nuclear configuration which he masters. Separation is the
modus vivendi of the system that has produced speculation and the
oedipal circuit. Displacement of *Hegueule* by a selfless, nomadic
Plusje is tantamount to an unbuckling of all the major orders of
sense we have inherited from the nineteenth century—the so-called
transparency of writing included. The effect is to turn the writer
into a producer of text-force unending in time, selfless in propriety,
and benevolent in dispensation of energy. Eradication of a central,
individuating being by means of its production of letters in terms of
ever-errant discourse where, above, every author-remover (*oteur*)
must jump-remove itself (*s'oter*) into his host-guest-author (*hotre*)
so that a named—limited, cited, positioned, univocal, and unilateral—son turns into a more incestuous no-child (*nonfils*) of du-
bious familial origin.[62]

Obviously, the consequence of sexual politics depends, à la
Joyce, on a confusion of the phonic and visual dimensions of writ-

ing. The duplicitous reading of words in paragrammar and anagram restores the veracity of the phantasm that transpires to the reader as a gift. The text before the eyes—between imaginary and real status, between a manifest and latent expression of the author—is an emergent, half-born form which, as lure of the desire of writing, must force the reader to desire to write. Since *Partie,* Cixous has written texts which are half-originary scenes. They body forth as a series of musical movements amplifying the fragments of life lived into a far more significant ensemble of given desires extended and repressed through the physical shape of the words. Her texts require a different reading process, for the book has not only a therapeutic function—the writer writing "out" of an exiguous or painful scene in the real in order to reduce meditation with an over-obstinate presence of practical, familial, or phallocentric thinking programming the mother—but also an instructively pleasurable configuration that releases the body from the seeming transparency of the mind, preempting desire. The texts unwind and spiral away from half-events or truisms, and leave in their motion traces of majestic psychic orchestrations.

3

Writing the Missexual: A Cleopatrician in Her Own Right

Write Yourself!

Cixous's most popular text, *La Jeune Née,* coauthored with Catherine Clément in 1975, marks a shift toward an overt feminine militancy. Cixous's part, "Sorties," replaces the patriarchal "know thyself" with a call to women to "write themselves." The call now addresses women, in the plural, as one of the terms in a binary configuration. The tone, still exuberant, becomes more defiant—toward men. Cixous continues the attack on Hegelian desire of recognition, the *Empire du propre,* and urges textual liberation through poetic writing in dialogue with philosophy and psychoanalysis. From a sovereign writing beyond coincidence of opposites, the emphasis shifts toward the notion of bisexual (missexual) writing: not one of two halves, but one in which the other sexual component is not repressed. Women, as many feminist rereadings of Freud's texts on hysterics assert, repress their other sexual components less than men.

"Sorties" and its follow-up, *La Venue à l'ecriture,* stage questions that each subject asks of (literary) history and is asked in turn by a real to which history both gives access and bars. How will woman enter on the scene of the real? She must think herself and think her power of action, of transformation, at the crossing of laws, of her desire. Like Freud's Dora, she must cut herself off from the laws (and the eye) of the master and throw herself into the movement of history, of the public. The texts are again texts of transformation, between fiction, psychoanalysis, philosophy, written there where writing stages itself, the way the real is always a theater, a locus where writing is carried off into history.

"Write yourself," is Cixous's call both in *La Jeune Née* and *La Venue à l'Ecriture*. This call is carried out in the fictional texts—*Souffles, LA, Angst*—where the endeavor is double: to re-traverse all the loci where women had been excluded (fiction, myth, psychoanalysis, and others) and to produce a subversive fiction that is not a representation of a real but a phantasmatic writing undoing censorship and repression, toward and from woman.

Le féminin futur: La Jeune Née

Displacing the "eternal" feminine, *La Jeune Née* announces a series of future feminist writings that will, like the texts of Cixous and Clément, surpass the limits of the narrowly ideological work of agonistic stamp characterizing much of the woman's liberation—writings that will appeal to genres of feminism unaware of the conceptual patterns dictating empirical practice.

In its physical shape, the book suggests what has been happening but has not been enunciated for a general public simply because habits of discourse and behavior have disjoined living from sensorial impressions. With Clément and Cixous, the *book* loses its insipidity as an object of consumption: it is projected as an aural prosthesis, a megaphone into which a masculine reader, like the RCA dog, is invited to plunge his nose and listen to another master's voice, a serenade whose sound no longer whistles but now charms and enchants. As Cixous has written it, the book is one of forebirth, an *introductio*. The text is pinpointed by its *blason*, ⋎ , illuminated in part by an inverted resemblance to the abstraction of the most commonplace of Parisian toponyms, the newly heraldic *tour effel*, cloturing *LA* in the vicinity of the Martial Fields. The tower's dramatic inner bends leave a brilliant center of light in the groins of the four beams of f-like legs on which the she-beast and shepherdess of Paris is poised: "I am ready to begin again, immediately. I raise my head. Up there, pink and veiled, above these urban cubes of a mediocre height, rises the Effelle Tower. It is from there (*là*) that we must throw ourselves."[1] Hence the person is born in the singular and the here and now (*là-je-une-nais*). In the exhilaration felt with the enunciation of *là je nais,* the speaker flexes her members in the discursive energies of a collective body, a feminine Leviathan.

A different woman comes everywhere to life. In the same manner the "young born" call to woman is an erasure of a constrictive paternity. The title, *La Jeune Née,* effaces the barriers by which categories of incest are bounded, making of the voice exclaiming its birth and separation a "mother born" who is a force of an "époux-mère," a fatherly mother-born neither instituting nor repeating the oedipal concepts of difference that, according to Clément and Cixous, inform (historically and etymologically) the *cliché* of woman: a hysterical, sorcerous, guilt-ridden being under the spell of the father.

Like the armories of the double *f,* the writing in both sections of *La Jeune Née,* in its configuration as a form of communication, deals with sexual adequation: that is to say, the condition of expression breaks, yet underscores, the constraints catalyzing it. The crude figure of the book itself is, like all the entries in "*Le Monde en 10/18*" series, ten by eighteen centimeters. Readers of the collection know, as do many of the authors, that "the world ten by eighteen" signifies many of the paradoxes of writing for a wide public. The books are manufactured cheaply and have no pretension beyond that of fulfilling a momentary need, as do the 10/18 volumes of transcribed lectures and discussions from Cerisy, Paris VIII, the *École normale,* and the like. And the numerous printers' errors, the vagaries of computerized type-setting, the unevenly distributed ink on sulfite paper, and the glue used in binding leave a great deal to be desired for those shelving and stocking the ideas of modernity. Once a "world ten by eighteen" is read, the book generally falls apart. Cixous and Clément realize this. They incorporate the tactile features of the text into its global process of meaning by forcing the unkempt aspects of the series—indeed any of its ideological contradictions in terms of the production of social change with the major organs of capital in Paris—to mirror themselves against the feminist endeavor. By publishing in the collection, they negate the negative side of buying, digesting, and giving birth to books; they bring the text as close as possible to the awareness of a primary process where contrary forces coincide. Cixous and Clément rejoice in the place where there has been a loss of aura and literature in the staggering growth of discarded ideas, in the economy of cheap texts and fatuous marketplaces like the FNAC.[2] In doing so, they underline a crisis of the writer: the distributing organs threaten to establish laws of taste over editors, authors, and readers. The woman writing today finds herself facing not three but four male-dominated institutions. The middleman has gained more power by negotiation than ever before.

Not unpredictably, Hubert Damisch has expressed guarded reserve about the massive ideological implication of cheap ideas—a reserve, however, that Cixous and Clément destroy much more flagrantly than Damish himself. "Man can be cultivated," he noted of the reading public, "bathed in culture as one says of a child swimming in language: he does not possess culture; and no institution, no industry could ever offer it to him, culture being no more, in its basis, than the work of appropriation ceaselessly recommenced, this always masked effort to surmount a distance, an alienation that pocket culture can feign to ignore but that it supposes as its very condition, and whose contours it reveals in its manners."[3] Where Damisch stockpiles his critique of book sales by transferring the statement from a review to a prestigious and expensive text of agglutinated articles, Cixous and Clément, mimicking this economy of repetition, invest themselves in a book of little substantial worth. Their gesture is more daring, "giving, giving, a spectacle against repetition of the spectacle."[4] They envisage the object as a feminized gift, a worthless, half-born shape; a word that in semiotic flow could be a half-symbolic present, a *donne,* a *gift,* and a gift-not (*don-ne*).

And so, in publishing an apparently hastily written piece, the authors surpass a masculine, perhaps gonocentric project of articulating ideas intended to go beyond the shape of the book and the bodies attached in signature. The tactic involves a paradox of irreconciliation between the theoretician and the artist. Clément unravels the binds of contradiction in the half-conscious associations of women with sorcery and hysteria from the Renaissance to modern times. How the mythology of the matrix—the lunatic—has been economized by means of popular idiom is the topic of her readings of psychoanalysis, the history of science and anthropology. Culpability serves in her study as a catalytic agent for the circulation of two sides of the same coin, the demonic creature outside the social order. Woman is the one who, once within, is literally ripped inside out. "She has become hysterical. As Dora's cough is a castrative response to the suitor's kiss, as the witch can lock the belt and sterilize man, in the same way, by anesthesia, the defensive, 'castrating' woman cuts herself away from the world of men. The freedom has become radical; separation irreversible."[5] In effect, this evidence drawn from various disciplines becomes in turn Cixous's cause, her text exemplifying the need for the female—whether "critic," "writer," "professor," "artist," or otherwise—to seize upon the movement of separation, that is to disjoin her expression from the econommimetic binds to which not only the female, but even Catherine Clément's discourse is attached. One half of *La Jeune Née* projects toward the ruse of the female phoenix fusing ridiculous binarities of oedipal culture, a spiraling *envol* of bisexual configuration; the second accedes to a discourse conflating oppositions in the movement of a prose expropriating the very categories that had accorded it the condition to write. Cixous's text involves loss in the generalized gift: "All is to come, aspiration, flight. The more you have, the more you give, the more you are, the more you give, the more you have."[6] In this passage, she must write by avoiding an explicative discourse building itself on reserve and difference, in a continually projective text.

Continuing her search for passages (*sorties*) out of a Hegelian system and phallogocentric entrapment, she denounces well-known hierarchical couples of opposites—man/woman, activity/passivity, sun/moon, culture/nature, day/night, father/mother, head/feeling, intelligence/sensibility, logos/pathos—and the primacy of form over matter: convex, walk, advance, sow, progress over concave, ground-on-which-one walks, receptacle.[7] These oppositions extend to the positioning of bodies in society and to the codification of sexual difference found in all symbolic practices: myths, legends, books, and major discourses governing society. The ordering of values (with their connotations of presence and substance) are accompanied by moral values, good or bad. The history of philosophy and literary history have always been read from a masculine point of view by men and women alike. The masculine edifice that passed for eternal and natural must be reread, and arbitrary privileges relying on the naturalization of the cultural must be displaced. Every story reduces woman to her body, the nonsocial, nonpolitical, acultural, listening to the sound of her inside, her "home." She is incapable of sublimation, immediately tuned into her affects, her appetites. In man's fiction and poetic myths, woman is always absent, hence desirable according to a logic of desire based on lack. To this (phallocentric) notion making of woman the domestic other, Cixous opposes woman as the "real" other, unknowable, nontheorizable, distant in her proximity.

The Question of a Feminine Bliss

The masculine statement must be questioned: "There are two irrepresentables, death and the female sex." Defiantly, Cixous urges a look at the Medusa: "She is beautiful and she laughs."[8] Laughter, a term absent from Hegel's discourse, shatters the negative moment of death and brings women to life and movement. Freud's reading of the myth, with his insistence on petrification as the moment of passage into a symbolism based on castration, is also mocked. Women must break out of silence and write. Thus they come onto the stage of a "real"; they affirm themselves beyond the negative moment of the hysteric who, rather than speak herself, remains spoken about. Cixous encourages women to engage in a writing practice, to tell from their border of a feminine "experience" which has been analyzed exclusively from the male side. Women must discover the locus of their *jouissance* (bliss) and inscribe its libidinal effects. Until now, the majority of writing has been done under the sign of castration. Some women—under pressure—have interiorized it and have crossed over to the masculine side. But how does castration affect women, what does it mean for women? How does it write itself? The feminine equivalent may be quite different. Women must ask themselves: "Who am I? How do I feel pleasure?"[9]

Metaphorization of Masculine and Feminine

In *La Jeune Née,* Cixous develops some theoretical points about the writing of sexual difference. Instead of a nominal difference (man, woman), she proposes using qualifiers (masculine, feminine), which, she insists, do not refer in an exclusive way to one or the other of the genders. "Masculine" and "feminine" function as differential predicates that can be used for men and women. There is no timeless essence of femininity and masculinity, only subjects caught in a network of historical power relations. All language is metaphoric, and abstract concepts are always used by those in power to insure their supremacy. Everything is language, and the body is always a written, never a "natural" body. The (political) economy of masculine and feminine is organized by different needs and constraints which, when they become socialized and metaphorized, produce signs, relations of power and production, a whole immense system of cultural inscriptions.[10] Cixous is beginning to theorize sexual difference into a difference of libidinal economies or drives. The term drive (*Trieb*) is itself a vague and problematic term in Freud, a "limit-term between the psychic and the somatic."[11] To remove it from the limit would mean to fall back into a facile biologism.[12] Freud hesitates: on the one hand, the drive is said to be a "psychic representative of excitations which—origi- nating in the body—have made their way into the soul";[13] on the other hand, the drive is represented by a representation (*Vorstel- lung*). "A drive can never become an object of consciousness, only the representation which represents it. Even in the unconscious, it cannot be represented other than through representation."[14] Freud's hesitation between drive as representing and represented shows that it is neither one nor the other, but both. It is determined as movement of representation, insofar as the latter is not grounded in the signified but produces meaning only as differing effects. This strange representation of a drive depends less on a content than on a process of articulation (primary process) in the unconscious. Cix- ous does not dwell on the difficulties (also pointed out by Lacan) inherent in the term but simply equates sexual life with libidinal economies or drives. For her, the most important question will be, how do drives write themselves, for men? for women?

After retracing the exclusion of woman through myth and liter- ary history, she asserts—in the wake of Nietzsche and contempo- rary readings of him—that there is no more destiny than nature or essence. One can not speak of *woman* or of *man* without being taken inside an ideological theater where representations of images, reflections, myths, identifications transform, deform, alter cease- lessly everyone's imaginary.[15] A freeing of the imaginary will trans- form behavior, mentalities. That is where fiction as projection into the *non-encore-là* is of strategic value.

Writing Sexual Differance

Cixous, in the post-1968 euphoria, urges women to imagine simul- taneously a general change in structures of education, training, re- production, and a real liberation of sexuality: that is to say, a transformation of the relationship of each to her (and his) body and to the other body. This cannot be done without political transfor- mations. Then, femininity and masculinity would inscribe other- wise their effects of difference, their economy, their relation to spending, to lack, to gift. What appears as feminine and masculine today would not come back to the same. Difference would not be based on opposition but on a bouquet of differences. But we still muddle, with a few exceptions, in the old.[16] Announced here briefly is a program of great breadth, hence some of the difficulties—beyond control—in its implementation. Insisting on the necessity of transforming individual, family, and society, Cixous will concentrate—within her self-established limit of artistic production—on the private sphere of individual and family rather than on the public sphere of the state. Her public contribution, as one of the founders of Paris VIII, concentrates on pedagogy in an effort to displace the rigid, hierarchical relationship between master and disciple, professor and student and to question the role of the institution.

Laws of society, through correct repression of drives, have divided individuals into men and women. "Nowadays, few are those who accept the uncertain beings on the side of poetry who admit the component of the other sex." Because, for Cixous, writing from the imaginary implies the invention of "other I's," the poet *is* more open to otherness. She follows the post-revolutionary myth of the artist as subversive and effeminate. Poetry, like other arts, questions and transforms ideology. "Only thus can one invent: thinkers, artists, creators of new values, 'philosophers' in the mad Nietzschean way, inventors and smashers of concepts, of forms, of life can only be agitated by singularities, complementary or contradictory. This is not to say that to create, one must be homosexual, but that there is no invention without other I's, no poetry, no fiction without that of a certain homosexuality, therefore of bisexuality."[17] Following the Nietzsche of *The Birth of Tragedy* and other early works, Cixous privileges metaphor.[18] Erasing the opposition between proper and metaphor, Cixous generalizes the use of the second term, which functions strategically and no longer rhetorically. Concept and identity give way to unending metamorphoses without a stable "I," where there is no more opposition between world and art, real and imaginary.

Between Freud and Nietzsche, from unconscious, dream, bisexuality, and metaphor, Cixous sings of bliss, energy, and love that bind and unbind amorous singularities. Bisexuality is not thought of as neutrality to castration, not as fusion of two into one, but as that with which each subject not enclosed in a false theater of phallocentric representation invests her erotic universe. There is inclusion in each, individually, of the presence diversely manifest according to each of both sexes, a nonexclusion of difference, hence a multiplication of effects and of inscription of desire on all parts of the body and on the body of the other. Classical psychoanalysis has to be questioned. Modern sexual difference is organized around the oedipal complex and castration, used to naturalize a cultural repression of woman. To say that in a certain way woman is bisexual is to displace and reopen the question of difference. Today, Cixous asserts, writing belongs to women, who are more open to bisexuality than men because of their cultural position. There is a certain slippage in Cixous's texts between the erasure of the concept "woman"—libidinal drives do not refer to one or the other of the sexes exclusively—and a return to woman. A new chain forms: women, bisexuality, artists, writing. Rereading, like other feminists,[19] Freud's remarks that woman is more open to bisexuality than man, Cixous concludes that woman is more open to otherness than man and should be urged to write: "Writing is the passage in me, entering and existing, the sojourn of the other who I am and am not, whom I do not know how to be but whom I feel going through me, who makes me live, tears me apart, disquiets, alters whom? one, some, several of the unknowns, who gives me the desire to know and from whom all life springs. This investment does not allow repose or security; it troubles always the relationship to the 'real,' produces effects of uncertainty which are obstacles to the socialization of the subject."[20]

The theoretical question for Cixous is, where in writing does difference pass? how do libidinal economies inscribe themselves at the level of artistic practice? Once again, it seems that the qualifiers "masculine" and "feminine" give way to the sexual bodies of man and woman, the more so as Cixous has recourse to traditional metaphors of women: diffusion, liquefaction, aerial swimming before the symbolic. Woman operates on the side of loss and spending, associated with life and force. The father is only a linguistic convention, but the mother *is* in body and name. She has a presence. The statement is important for her future writings. It is because of her proximity to the body that woman's writing is close to voice and rhythm (*rhythmos,* a respiration, an exhalation, a breath of life, *souffle*). This rhythm makes the text heave, rends it with shrieks, or composes it of silences. Cixous "valorizes" what had been decried for centuries: woman materializes with her flesh, signifies with her body what she thinks. Her discourse, even "theoretical" or political, is never simple, linear, or "objective"; she drags into history her history.[21] Discourse, theory, and logic on the side of the concept, science, and truth are for Cixous—as for many male thinkers— reappropriating and establishing power structures. Yet Cixous, through her gender distinction, adds a further division, which, though caught in a historical configuration, runs the risk of becoming another conceptual opposition. Aware of the danger, Cixous insists that a writing of the feminine must remain exorbitant and avoid enclosing itself in another totalitarian "ism." And in the wake of the German Romantics, she adds: "Women like disquiet, questioning. There is waste in what we say. We need waste. To write is always to break the exchange value which keeps the word on its rail, to give its savage part to abundance, to uselessness."[22]

From the self-engendering virgin maiden of *Le Troisième Corps,* Cixous shifts to a revalorization of the mother as presence through voice but before the name. What never ceases to resonate in feminine writing, she claims, is that which, having traversed women erstwhile, touches them imperceptibly, profoundly, and keeps the power to touch them: the song, the first music, that of the first voice of love which every woman keeps alive, contrary to men, for whom the source is continually cut off.[23] The mother's voice, at the same time interior and exterior, never accedes to a perception. It does not appear on stage. Cixous shifts away from a theater of eyes toward a problematic of voice, music, tone. Close to Nietzsche's song of the world, Cixous finds the "origin" of song and poetry in the mother's voice. In this period of feminist militancy, writing shifts more and more toward a search for the origin. The mother's voice sings before the law. Contrary to the father, who is exterior, the mother as intimate addressee is always "present," refuses separation. She opens onto language. "She is that which between you spaces you and pushes you to inscribe in your language and style of woman."[24] Against Freud's oedipal theories, Cixous asserts that the woman is never cut off from her mother. The absent, lost mother must be found again. She has to be read outside a cultural role, as non-name, as non-proper, and as source.

Women have almost everything to write of femininity: of their erotization, their pleasures and sexuality. To date, only the hysterics have opposed phallocentric desire. They are, in Cixous's terms, forerunners of the new women; hence the importance of Dora in some of Cixous's writings. Yet like other literary and mythological figures, she cannot be erected into a truth. Cixous must leave her and go on to another figure.

From the drunken artistic writing of the world, the emphasis shifts to a freeing of cultural repressions through a bisexual writing as close as possible to an unconscious. In writing, Cixous states, women will realize an uncensored relationship to their being-as-woman. "Write yourself; your body must be heard. Then will spring forth the immense resources of your unconscious."[25] The unconscious, associated with wealth, abundance, is opposed to the conscious as poverty and repression. At the intersection of Freud and Nietzsche, Cixous urges *women* to undo cultural and personal repressions through writing, a writing at the same time gender- and nongender-oriented.

Sein

Traversing a cumulus of genuinely masculine theory on the binary unity of the sign and Hegelian *Empire du propre,* based on the master/slave rapport, Cixous at this stage centers it all on the mother's breast, *sein,* figuratively the bosom, center, the core of being: *sein* in its Germanic heritage, the whole body of metaphysics, but dull, absorbent, a deadened object of little value in human exchange as a territory desired by another body, itself less the cohesion of hill and valley in metaphors of convexity than a salubrious menstrual *seing* (signature, stamp) of flowing forms and an empty thing, a philosophical copulative, a *sein* ringing harmonic difference. The bosom accedes to the equivalent of copy, a proliferated text that in every advertisement is veiled to catalyze a continually frustrated exchange. As the foremost stereotype among popular phantasms, the breast must predicate everywhere an imagined need for bodily fulfillment. In collusion with the etymon of *cliché* and *clicher* (an onomatopoeia stamped from the noise of a matrix falling on molten metal) as a solid, hard plate in the typographer's studio from which infinite identities can be made, the breast in Cixous's vocabulary is sensationally flat. Its failure to evoke, that is to represent, the palpable object of desire locates that of a more ebullient and—in ideological terms—far more transgressive area in which all sexual difference and institutionalized eroticism have fallen. Unlike French blazoneers such as Clément Marot and Pierre de Ronsard, who described Platonic perfection in the balance of double and marbrine balls, with her flat chest Cixous seeks an adamic state of trance in the inadequate weight of the word and body: the *sein,* like its spectacular shape, is both hollow and full, ponderous and airy, one and the other, a sign of separation where, in a sort of white writing, the nipple continually congeals the scar of something pulled away from it, missing the point of contact that has to be phantasmatically reattached to other nipples in order to pattern a matrix and puncheon of missexual writing designing the ideogrammatic *chi,* the χ or analogue in the Chinese 夂.

Cixous argues for a future feminism across Kleist and Shakespeare. "Kleist is Penthesilea. The same needs that cannot stay closed in the limits of any being whatsoever, the same spurting grandeur that wants to appear, mix her fire with the daylight, even eclipse the sun, which no one can contain in her breast: he who can desire nothing but her."[26] In blending with the tale of Achilles and Penthesilea, Cixous embodies a rapture and seizure where Amazons gather up men like roses, dominate their former dominators in order to efface the space of mastery, literally to kill bellicose force so that the thrust of love can be communally freed. Penthesilea and Cixous are, however, neither camouflaged soldiers in khaki nor *guerillères,* since the martial female in their view is nothing but a "woman who has killed the woman in her,"[27] coming into femininity only by death and still more sexual opposition. The victorious loss of division comes when the heroine removes her cuirass, belt, and holster, when she can "descend into her own breast where Achilles is torn apart."[28] In the meeting of the hollow bosom and the emasculated genitals, Cixous finds the model of a separatist unity. This is what she had earlier called "buckling the buckle"[29] or going around the world in a figured asymptosy. In literature, this was represented by the marionettes whose strings are joined to an authorial hand, and where there is established in the distance of translation between their cardboard autonomy and the fingers of the puppeteer a mobile sense of play and a loss of both authority and originality. A dramatically autonomous machine takes over control of language.

On these threads Cixous ends her portion of *La Jeune Née* with the drama of Cleopatra, who in her eyes is a model from which future feminism can be reproduced. Because the queen knew how to give herself to the eye in her attire, comportment, and body, the Shakespearean version of the heroine surpassed the ocular limits of masculine and feminine habit that would see in the other a dazzling light, a darkened continent, or "the blind spot of an old dream of symmetry."[30] She refuses to see male/female relations in terms of the magnetics of complementarity that has determined most discourse around men and women. Cleopatra is "profusion, energy, exuberance,"[31] and incorporates a triply negative, supremely lucid envelopment of desire and language embracing separation: "But Cleopatra has the strength of will to master the space-ment [the spacing, that is, the spatial lie that separates masculine from feminine], fills up with her flesh, with her outstretched senses, the hole in love, and however far away he (Antony) is, it is still in her that he is, that he is felt. . . . In truth they discovered together the admirable resource of sanctity."[32] This collapse of distance in desire and feeling marks the condensation of near-simultaneous readings following the rhythms of English and French.

In alluding to Shakespeare—and she has repeatedly admitted a preference for him over Joyce—Cixous appeals to a supple, pre-Cartesian mold of language richer in associative range and far more cohesive in sensorial substance of flesh and word than fiction that attempts to feign a valiant retrieval of symbol across the doctrinal divisions of word and thing. Her assertive passages, like that above, cannot be decrypted until the reader's desire to capture an always fleeing stability of ambiguity is suspended and converted into a will to inhabit words, to experience the flight. In the rereading, Cleopatra's *mastery* is a deception of a master, just as her senses seem to be firm concavities of withoutness seen from within. In her progress toward the keynote term *sainteté*, the sentence looks the vault of its ambiguous architectonics. Teasingly, the *sens* and *trou* hover between sense and breast, truth and vacuity; the diction couples the lovers in question by final insistence on sanctity, a connotation of sexual loss in apotheosis, yet also a retrieval of the trance of the bodies finding their most communicative rhythm, on the level of the signifer, in a suggestion of breasts crossing and caressing each other, lips sucking nipples of indeterminate gender.

In a position akin to that of Derrida's texts since *La Dissémination*—expanding and contracting its own semantic network—Cixous's text and its forebears stomatically open and close their verbal epiderm according to varying degrees of corporeal strength that the reader can bring to them. But inevitably the books reveal the ideological tropisms of those who cannot help reacting either positively or negatively to them.[33] Written to build a great body of changing sensibility projecting from 1976 to the future, their integuments have been decorated according to the needs of the woman's market. The result is that the perspective has a Shakespearean quality in its coextension with the human form, displaying at given moments differing degrees of erogenous charge, certain passages releasing tremendous affective energies willing to embrace the text, others soliciting reduced desire, others leaving sensations of temporary indifference.

The reaction to Cixous in the United States will be a capital test indicating the corporeal status of textual and ideological freedom in feminist writing. Those dismissing her (unfortunately) reveal the sadness of a bodily lack as well as a timidity at the thought of having to leave the paradise garden of theoretical discourse on women. Those reacting favorably will in turn refuse to be part of a romanticized schizophrenia, and by mere affirmation will manifest a desire to reinvent language where the female can speak in and outside the molds of reason and folly. Again, Cixous does favor a future feminism nourished on the concepts and problematics of Freud. She asks how, in effect, feminism can turn psychoanalysis toward the woman rather than against, as psychoanalytic practice has done heretofore, owing to deficient conceptual rigor and lack of textual acuity. The first step taken by Cixous is to write in the "name" of the mother, in a name that does not name, with white ink flowing from an interior breast.

Cixous's distance from any established pattern of militant writing may be pinpointed in the recurrent motif of *vol*—flight and theft—in *La Jeune Née* and *LA,* a book on feminine dreams. The motif invokes and inscribes a transgressive gesture whose articulation comes as close as any to going beyond practical limits in the empirical domains of reading and living. Cixous coins and spends words literally outside the space of meaning, at once regressing to the kind of infantile expulsion that some theoreticians have demarcated, and projecting ahead and over the locus of sense. This can be partially elucidated by reference to Freud's own hesitations, substitutions, and continually remodeled association of a primary process with condensations of constraints. The other, negative side of expression repressed from meaning finds itself not anagrammatically but homonymically destructive of the perimeters to which the word points. Strategically denying Freud the calm of an etiquette like "repression"—expressed by the acquisition of a contrary meaning "where contraries come together" and where, in the unconscious, there exists no "no" in the explanation attenuating the violence of contrariety—Cixous pushes ahead. She accumulates distortions to the verge of an emblematic prose, a text profusely riddled with displacement of meaning.

Paradoxically it all holds together. Against a type of feminist writing that defers its impact by staging scenes beyond the interlace of words, always going below their habitual folds of meaning, *La Jeune Née* ubiquitously insists on itself *en vol*—in flight, yes, but also in effraction, love and theft at once signifying an all-in-nothing. The ruse of an absent E apocopated from V/O/L is one where "the woman takes from the bird and from the thief as the thief takes from the woman and the bird: the wingies [*illes*] pass the wingies run."[34] Or in *LA*, Cixous designates a group of women (presumably working together at Paris VIII) who will "spread on their hills and coast a rain of thieving verbal images [*une pluie d'images verbales volantes*]."[35] It is a question of menstrual molting, a way to "contaminate" genders and numbers in passing from one side to the other by "enchantment, infantment, or *enjambement*, of throwing a verbal lay [*un pont verbal*] between desires and realities."[36] Superimposed over *La Jeune Née*, the birth in *LA* does more than recall Cleopatra. The half-born maiden is evident in the snake emerging from the shell, the very creature who will fly on the head of a triumphant Medusa and who will caress the breasts of the North African queen: the ensign of a radical critical aspiration.

Certainly in Cixous's eyes, the push to break out of an analytical space in modern writing—to teach "how" to read Mallarmé, Freud, Joyce, Derrida without insistence on the woman from the woman's body—cannot but be a tautological error. Already her espousal of separation across the flight and larceny of letters puts in question and then forecloses the self-castratory gesture of any given critical method said to engender new life in an old fiction. In the figure of a game of hearts, Cixous shoots the moon: she acquires the queen of spades (known as the old whore) and then amasses all the tricks to the detriment of those playing with her. In one example, a section of *Partie*, she takes up theories explicitating post-1890 writing and a concept behind much post-1970 fiction, where a pre-oedipal, semiotic moment of flow is supposedly occulted by the complementary, divided signs of an Occidental sociality, and where the impetus of the scriptor is to reinject the freedom of movement across the constraints of symbolic systems of order. By doing so, she encircles and disintegrates the limits of strategies miming a deferred recuperation of the so-called speaking subject (for example, "I think my mother, therefore I am"). The supple torsions in her text parody originary theories that are supposed to lead semiotics out of an impasse. Her force is but treacherously rendered in translation:

And the interfellation would have spurting over the preceptacle in void a melange of virgital, mineral, and denimale isolutions of oil or ink or ficture or other countermilks, unreadable, splashing and insextinguishable.

Yet from the point of view of Alybido ridendi, one must avoid interpreting this lubrifission of incuntinuity under pain of curdling the fluidity, of screwing it, or riveting in order to milk it.

For one would fall into the acadermic breaksheet, which is of a pair with the paranoia of this very devine: from a certain blind spot the devine would be dying to be intercepted and sexplicated and to lose a drop of his essence.[37]

Cixous writes a text fending itself from the economies of a metalanguage, but by all available means displaces some formerly "deconstructive" metaphors that have become feminist slogans. The temper of the word is struck in a way to defy calculated appropriation by any single group, a metaphysics of duality, or a school of uterine origin and hysterical beginning that was essential to certain readings of philosophy and psychoanalysis. Her praxis in its reconstruction of the female cause has uncanny resemblance to that of Derrida projecting his own work in terms of the specific *négoce* (commerce) of performing writing in a pedagogical and ideological situation. With hers, like his, "the incalculable must be of the other *partie.* The unreceptible—what takes at a determined moment the informed form of the unreceptible—can, even ought, at a determined moment, not be received at all, can escape from the criteria of receptibility, be totally excluded from what can take place in daylight, though when the unreceptible product circulates from hand to hand."[38] The part is justly what cannot receive, but in being lamentably irrecuperable, arrives best in giving loss.

Thus *Partie,* in its parity of divided typeface and inverted halves of *Si-je* and *Plus-je,* must strategically defy a stamp of nefarious complementarity, a thetic basis in front of a *chora,* anti-oedipal paradigmatics, antifetishism, hysteria-cum-matricality, the double knot of the modern female, all bandied theories that Derrida again—in reference to *Glas,* with which *Partie* has a certain congruence—puts in the brackets of "tattooed processions, incised, incrusted on the body of two colossed piers or two bands, one agglutinated, tressed, at the same time gripped to the other and slipping over the other, in a dual unity and without rapport to itself."[39] The reading of *Partie* derives from the intercolumnar loss in the mode of a language doubly and singly adequate to the woman, between imposing piers of philosophy, psychoanalysis, and literature. Yet *La Jeune Née* serves well as the most cogent prolegomenon in its erasure of the hyphens or bars between male female, master slave, criticism fiction, in order to give way to an infinite play of difference(s).

Put another way, the text has an effect similar to the ideographics of Cixous's preface to the French translation of Phyllis Chesler's *Women and Madness,*[40] visibly erasing the difference between French theory and American practice of feminism. Cixous inserts herself between two categorical imperatives: the difference between, on the one hand, an American empiricism in a clinical history of the institutionalized female represented by Chesler's text, and on the other hand, a study of the logic of repression, Derridean in its lineaments, held by Luce Irigaray. How to make the two views converge was and still is an important problem. Will American women, the introduction asks, ever come to situate repressions in

the realm of speech acts, in matrices of binary thinking always behind the words describing and copying liberation? But all must be
done without impairing a valuable sense of alterity which can in no
way be recuperated by masculine reason. In brief, the otherness of
the female must be valorized so as to break the age-old distinctions
of intelligence versus sensuality, reason versus poetry, and male versus female at the same time that the floating missing signification of
no known attribute must be the non-essence of the female body.
Scripting her introduction to the French edition of Chesler, Cixous
tempers the theoretical and practical views, opting for a space of
forceful antheriority.

The Missexual

It may be that the resolution of a discourse sufficient to the other
finds its most dazzling effect in an issue of the review *Poétique* (of
which Cixous is both a founder and editor), in the components of a
missexualité. The issue tellingly demonstrates through this notion
how exclusion of the other sex would be contrary to the totalized
miss, a feminist praxis of writing on the crease of alterity, of a critical fiction or of fictional criticism. In the preface explaining why
the marquee:

> Finnegans Wake
> Number Composed by Hélène Cixous

is as it is,[41] the editor indicates how eight articles, mostly of Anglo-
French orientation, exploit four median pages (162–66) of the
novel. Cixous sits over the number of *Poétique* like a new Natura
over the wheel of life: when chance dictates the crisscrossings and
divergences among the seven critics—all men—they find themselves not explicating *Finnegans Wake* but rounded up in the pigsty
of Ulysses. A sort of editorial Circe, Cixous shows how, in brilliant
theatrics, the falsely ecumenical phrases of the critics predate her
style of analysis:

It has been decided to slip into *FW*, in a sort of text where in the emulsion of signifiers, it is His story which makes the most obvious signs. Letting oneself be traversed by a tongue with a thousand tongues in which His story stutters its nightmares [*Histoire balbutie ses cauchemars*] at the moment of the ide(a)s of Marge.

That gives [*donne*] the composed reading which follows. The "chance," that is, the contained extravagance of *FW*, has made it such that singular approaches—each of the players of this *partie* being free to seduce himself by the siren of his choice or to resist it—have traced roads which cross without barring or repeating each other, the whole drawing like a long phrase, an exquisitely bizarre rebus.[42]

The "marginal" readings for which each of the men felicitates himself by prestigious entry into the review is turned into a space of critical hogwash. It must be remembered that the road to titular success in the economy of acumen since 1970 has been gauged by the efficacity of traversal across ideas and oceans; an American writing in French on human sciences and literature or a Frenchman writing on neomodern Anglo-Saxons has been a sign of success that *Poétique* has exploited to maintain redoubtable prestige. This is less true of sexes and bodies. Effracting the exchange value of the review, Cixous dons the attire of an effete editor but, beneath the critical order of a Joycean siren, displaces masculine enunciations; the nightmares of History for the authors resemble the image of the young-born outlined in *La Jeune Née:* at once a sea and a mother-birth, a *couchemer* that expulses His stories and His critical vibrations in favor of a newer, embryonic form that she calls—tying together the loose ends of her writings on feminism—a great *MM* melting in the mouth, the goodness of a fake *bon-bon* refusing its degradation into a *bonne-bonne* (a maid-maid) through the resurgence of a *mère née* (a mother born) accouched in youth:

The omission of Miss M, at repeated intervals in *Finnegans Wake*, relates to the process of a placing into circulation by the text itself, in the mode of a projection (secretion, excretion, operation, re-apparition), of an

M-same [*M-même*], extirpating itself from the matrix like the first missive saved from the shit by the original hen [*la poule originale*] (*FW* III), the hen, mother-born, made to lay and nest the letter-eggs and propagate—the species already always spaces where the language writes itself and gives itself to be read.[43]

Allusion to a text written "in the 'name' of the mother" counterpoints the paternal line of reasoning maintained by adepts of a certain psychoanalysis who have seen the scriptural act motivated by a man for and against an omniscient father. Along these lines the "composed reading that follows" is no doubt engendered by the eye, the pupil, the look of a forceful Cixous who has joyously contained all of the men in her linguistic pouch, now slipping them in and out of the review's once academic volume as a parodic piece of criticism.

In this manner the subtitle of the issue, *Fort-sein,* becomes a very healthy mammary of being; it embodies the chiasmatic and oscillatory rhythms of a reader's desire to break out of the standardized oedipal model marked in *Sein.* She refers in part to the Derridean *seing* struck in *Glas* and the enclosure of a fortified inner space which gives, then milks the Odyssean men for their worth. Metamorphosed into pigs, they pass into Circe's stockyard and fall into the trap. All the men come to and from docile series of transitives placed between the brackets Cixous has marked between the *Fort-sein* (page 131) and the *Missexualité* (pages 240–49), which delineate the perimeters of the volume. The men speak intelligently and reasonably, as they have for centuries. Whence: "the Joycean text is like a fragmented body" (page 132); "writing is in effect produced like death" (page 176); "the text of Joyce in general, and *Finnegans Wake* in particular, overflows—is calculated to overflow—all discourse of knowledge, all scientific or philosophical discourse" (page 180); "whereas in most texts this figure that Genette calls the *narrataire* remains implicit, in *Finnegans Wake* the manipulations and enigmas of the text come back to the reader. In order that it be thus, in order that the experience of reading may become an active participation, it is necessary that the text present itself in an apparent disorder" (page 207). The enumeration of academic copulatives is exemplary of a writing necktied by a tradition that the missexual gap—here a negatively matrical format Cixous offers at the beginning and ending of the number—will serve to bring out its platitude.

She assigns herself a prosthetic task in the contribution entitled "La Missexualité." Following the asymptotic contours of the inner breast and the Cleopatrician phantasm elaborated in *La Jeune Née,* Cixous writes a marginal text uplifting the collegiate sag in the middle of the issue by compressing the midriff bulge so characteristic of most masculine writing in Joyce studies. The missexuality, drawn from a midsection, the middle of linear thinking, the median point between A and Z as the navel of the alphabet and the interior margin, will in her eyes espouse a freely militarized feminism, a locus in the middle-of-the-bed which has no real counterpart in American movements. Her ms. spots a miss to which Joyce accedes only in *Finnegans Wake.* But she had already noted this point at the end of *Prénoms de personne.*

It might be called an aesthetic of recuperative colossality, a seduction, theft, and appropriation of formerly worthless signifiers that men have wasted in their midst. She takes Joyce's sentence "Margareena she's very fond of Burrus" and uses it missexually. "Once more opposition butter masculine solid—tea liquid—a/lick, a/lack, she licks, she lashes, she lets, she lacks. *Shes velly fond of chee*—influence of the 'Eastasian import': she touches the tongue as an organ of taste, and in provoking phonic mutations and dissociations, transformations. Cheese divides and *a partie* becomes tea: *chee à la chinoise,* or even spirit (*chi*)."[44] The margin, a significant emulsion, is a prosthesis of butter, an artifice of margarine which in both the novel and critical context lubricates the passage of emasculated signifiers from banal words of reasoned (male) literature into artificial organs. The syntagmatic *chee/tea* encircles the ideogram of *chi,* signifying food as well as butter cookies on French coffee tables, the far more characteristic semaphores of the Franco-American biscuit labeled LU, an *elle eut,* and a shortbread from Nantes said to melt in the mouth; and even more obviously, she harks to the butter from Burrus, whose authenticity and originality are soured by the presence of the cheaper spread branded *Planta,* found in any French supermarket, replacing the "very picture of a needless woman,"[45] imprinted in every consumer's mind with the rosy-cheeked child holding a buttered slice of country bread in the cliché of *Elle (&) Vire,* a Norman butter of the first growth now applied over Joyce to signify the necessary turn, the *virage and virago,* that the future feminist must take in her missexual movement.[46]

The lack and miss of the words are simply too fattening for an intelligent reader, too slippery for hermeneutic or even paragrammatical absorption. Implicit allusion to the duplicative process in the printing of wrappers devalues the content of fat—a typically male problem—as a name and globule of energy, for among the hilarious clichés of French and American *emballage* issues the stereotype Cixous puts in the scission between herself and Joyce: the buxom milkmaid, the dairymaid, the coppermaid scrubber, the rubbermaid kitchen stopper, the orange minutemaid, and the raisined sunmaid who carry their pails and platters as artificial extensions of the two breasts which the patron fondles in the aisles of a self-service store to the somnolent tunes of Muzak. The *military young female* with all the lactic attributes the novelist had invested in her is momentarily bereft of plenitude in the crossing of plastic icons and litters of semantic association.

The allusion to *chee* in the context breaks the limits of the Joycean model, using for its own ends the *chi* stolen from Jacques Derrida, the subject of diverse pages of *Glas* and of the essay prefacing lithographs by Valerio Adami: "+R *(par-dessus le marché)*".[47] Inflecting cheese and rancid butter with indication of remiss of meaning and lack of taste insofar as the product turns to refuse, the *chee* cuts across the parabolic curvature of the woman's inner breast. Derrida had marveled, "*Reste—à savoir—ce qui fait chier,*"[48] an elegantly bizarre rebus of a who asking to see why the eating, crossing, shitting, and chirping (*qui-chi-chie*) of an excretory eye (*Ich*) might fall into a receptacle of meaning. The chiasm of body and language is in Cixous's version a copulative and a near-juncture of the Chinese and Greek *chi* drawn over the female, χ, phantasized as the meeting of two, even four breasts. The sign also connotes an intersective nipple in the center of Paris, again the *tour effelle*. Her *chee à la chinoise* pays homage to the grammaphonic corpus that had sought recovery of the unspoken body of modern letters.

The author finds it all in her name and in the vagaries of formerly cryptic thievery. But by far the most resounding critical thrust in the words is to be located in their dispersion. Cixous encourages students and readers to associate their impressions with those of the text. In this instance, we can essay the force of the allusion to margarine by means of its ideological prominence in circles of American taste. No doubt the most immediate connection would involve reference to *The Last Tango in Paris,* where Marlon Brando corners Maria Schneider. Where an intelligent public seized upon the spread as a sign of the torturous sense of communication in a fortyish misogynist, the impact of Cixous's signifier, borrowed from the annals of Jean Genet's years in prison and Derrida's transposal of their agony on the right column of *Glas,* tends to curdle the whole semantic emulsion of the film as it was received in America. The continental public was no doubt capable of seeing Orphic patterns of myth structuring the film,[49] but the American reaction was less congruent with its typological lines than the visceral reaction to the images without mediation by either language or intellect. At work was an American tendency to avoid the interference of classical myth, to fold anal eroticism into the image of margarine with the simulacrum of men's corn oil (notably "Fleischmann") across the genre of the bad joke. Their punch lines derive from a conceptual, historical hate of *both* the masculine and the feminine body—remembered along country roads in the buttering corn from the loins of the farmer's daughter—that structures any reaction to the film. The crisscrossing of impressions becomes so pastelled that the references to butter in "La Missexualité" even put in question the onomastic features that have molded generations of American antifeminists at the crucial sign of the letter M: for one, Marlon Brando splintering into Marlo Brandon, even Marl Brandiron, always imagined as a former hoodlum in a Nazi uniform of *The Wild Ones,* an overmale hero crossed and struck by an errant tire iron, who twenty years later rejuvenates his lost generation at Wounded Knee, less for love of an other sex or race than for the retrieval of his prosthetic trophy. By releasing, separating, and literally freeing the overconnoted signifier or hollow phallus among her readers and her text, Cixous calls for a productive use of the collective phantasm to sidestep an impeding mass of theoretical apparatus that would have excluded the contiguous associations of continental myth and bodily fears, even those including the figure of a mouth ingesting hot buttered popcorn as the eyes ogle the rampant sexism of the *Last Tango.*

A last, possibly unconvincing, attempt to present the deconstructive force of Cixous's signifier and to conclude with remarks in deference to her writing a half-born reflection: in the article on Joyce, Cixous's reference to Burrus is linked to, then rescinded from, Caseous in *Finnegans Wake.* She notes:

Thus with Burrus and Caseous, who, as we learn, affront each other for the mastery of his misstery: of what is made its misstery? The secret of imperial power is in the margin between Miss and miss.

The Missexuality of the maiden is also the checkmate [*l'échec*], the very name of the limit referring the emissary to himself. It is she who is the mastriss of the misters. A cleo/patrician in her own right, she at once complicates the position while BC are contending for her misstery

by implicating herself with an elusive   miss
Antonius   mastery
                                        mystery
                                       masteric[50]

But Cixous cannot dwell even on this summit of missexual writing, of subversion of codes and conventions, literary and academic; she pushes ahead, through more writing to come.

The Uncovery of a Feminine Language: La Venue à l'ecriture

"When I do not write, I feel as if I were dead," states Cixous in an interview on April 9, 1976, published in *Le Monde* a few months after the publication of *La Jeune Née*. Rather than insisting on an exchange of words in an efficiently communicative context, she appeals to supple rhythms of the written word which she asks the reader to feel and understand at once in order to decenter the privilege of voice which in the Judeo-Christian world has devolved from the authority of a god or father. She invokes a conceptual, unconscious totality from which speech emerges. Her writing wills to cross that threshold by an adamant insistence not on the myth of a feminine language but on an entirely scriptive activity having use only in the elaboration of a huge body of glyphic words assuring the promotion of a woman's cause in the drama of life—and not of life *and* letters.

Cixous enumerates an act at once naming and erasing, fraying the path of its own works, moving from binarity to creation, life-and-fiction, life-like-fiction, oedipal myth, castration complex, literary creation. An ultimate, tonic term in her phrase, *literature* irrupts from the difference bound to copulas which a vocative form has needed for its order. Whence the written text supersedes the echo of a suppliant, tortured voice of a female held in phallogocentric economies of representation.

Mater X

For the female, the printed text must be at once laboratory, workshop, forum, and nuptial chamber. Dissemination, a concept otherwise unjustly labeled as "masculine" among readers of Derrida's collection of essays of that title, is the basis for Cixous's coming to writing. In *La Venue à l'ecriture*, the next (and last?) in the series *féminin futur,* Cixous appropriates and formulates the concepts of the production of an ambiguous writing in order to propulse careers of feminist writers in collective fashion. She exploits her name as headline and symbolically gives birth to other women; the printed page as dead-born form assures the life of its author and is put on the market with no exchange or use value other than the release of the repressions of the author herself.

This is indeed a radical move. Cixous's attitude toward the process of purchase, reading, and critical commentary of books suggests that the long-founded notion of the *honnête homme* (or *honnête femme*) has to be disbanded once and for all. Because the drive to write and read must have a resourcefully strong narcissistic element, which paradoxically moves the person from the cultural repressions to a self-monitored opening and closing of her own writing body, the reader-writer must buy and sell texts for self-esteem and self-pleasure. Hence a wager *not* to purchase trends of critical formulations at about fifteen dollars per copy outside of a pattern dictated by the groupuscular unit of *le féminin futur.* The person-of-letters no longer informs herself. Form is already there, held in the universal uterus which is the commanding structure and force of production; she holds absolute preeminence over the phallus which, as stylus, can only try to mark the global shape of a matrix. Women, Cixous implies, have devalorized the uterus simply by molding it again and again, remolding it according to the classical binarity of stamp and puncheon or typeface and page that has determined sexual difference in the whole tradition of humanism that males have proffered since the twelfth century. To inform us is to deform a shape, once and for all, for the writing female is an all-and-all, a whole from which language is born over and over again. She hints that the matrix is opposite to the father who in oedipal psychology is the cause and effect of frustration, permitting hieratic communication and social relation to perpetuate themselves. Coined in a way like a "mater X," the woman's body with a sufficiency that the phallus lacks, has to show its disseminatory power through unending production of *texte.* For the woman the book is so fecund and so ubiquitous it has literally only to inundate with its amniotic flow of words.

Exhaust—Excise Tax

Flooding the market with words entails a strategy of forcing a play of catch-up or of difference on the part of the *honnête homme* or archi-reader. The feminist writer forces the outcome of the game of fiction at the inception of its rules, for in giving birth to one book after another, she exhausts the reader, who is plunged into the circuit of having to account always for that which supersedes a text just read. In a sense, she pushes the capitalist system to its horrendous outcome. The advantage for the female writer lies in the center of production. Because the "future feminists" elaborate the texts collectively, and because they contribute together to the endeavor of a matrical fiction, the product—as well as its inner logic and tissue of phantasms—has already been felt and read.

Now, the enterprise would seem chimerical, and it would—as we shall see—be that were it not for Cixous's position at Paris VIII. At the *Centre de recherches en études féminines,* the class she offers on feminist writing is the "factory of phantasm." There, in a neo-Freudian manner derivative of the methodologies of the *Traumdeutung,* women can write, paste together, mock up, and finally publish texts born of this interaction and exchange. *Scenes* are spoken, noted, transcribed, juxtaposed, and rewritten. Cixous repeatedly offers coursework on the theme of separation through which the articulations are passed. In part, the result is for the reader on the outside unreadable, ununderstandable, and meaningless insofar as it has no part in the world of *vouloir-dire* (meaning). In texts like *LA,* the dream writings are so profusely adumbrated that no one can, as perspicacious critic, ever *penetrate* the text with stylistic acumen. In reading, the male is left exhausted, excised, taxed to a resultant degree of realizing the limits of an intellectual economy of letters in the marketplace.

Fur Coat—Leather Belt

Since Freud, psychoanalysis has shown the twentieth century that texts are everywhere, ubiquitous, and if not meaningful in the amorphous space of the world, then born of a chaos which the perceiver wills to order. Part of Cixous's strategy of production depends on violent coincidence of "difference" in the matrix of fiction. At the former Vincennes, in a school notorious for a certain regal squalor—windows fissured, chairs piled helter-skelter in corners, posters stapled in magnificent collages of spectral filth over walls and windows, serving as milieu for an outstanding faculty of generally left-wing thinkers—Cixous used to enter the complex in a dazzling ermine coat whose capital worth most probably surpassed the means of many in the classroom. Her proxemics marked a progressive use of repression. As a replica of Bataille's evocation of Aztec ceremony, she surged from the context of the cheaply reinforced concrete of classroom shelters. She then became a surplus value and a zero-degree term, the sovereign center of a decorous, eminently caressive body where her politics splintered those of an archaic scene in which the king would have his wives circulate about him. Because of the rite of such a scene, which leads to writing on the part of all participants, Cixous's subjects celebrate her gift of energy materialized in the notes taken on the phantasm and published in *LA* as festive fragments elaborated from scenes heralding points of the female body.

I want *vulva*. Let her pronounce my names and I have! Let her read the book of my parts, and myself I advance with the book of my body in my mouth, and in my mouth I contain the volume that she travails [*oeuvre*] for me. If the following words go out of my mouth I will be able to see my Earth in mixing myself with my living beings, my corporeal powers will cede to no eclipse, eternally, and all she speaks is made beautiful from my tongue's point of view: "*Vulva!*"[51]

In pretext of her classroom, she enacts the release of the name from its phantasm in italics above to its Roman splendor when, at the beginning of every seminar, she unbuckles her belt: a half-cuirass. Her strap frees the body and disintegrates the militant or civic order of the practical world; this is indeed a sensuous militancy that calls her audience to write both with and against the male, to write when the strap undoes the pressures needed to protect and chastize the uterus in the male order. Such are the lures of a modern Cleopatra, a magnanimous neo-Natura who forces the woman in writing to unbuckle the clothing with which she has had to be preserved.

Vermeer Mhysteria

Part of the argument for a women's discourse depends on what she construes to be the ever gravid shape of writing. Cixous's markedly feminine works such as *La Jeune Née, La Venue à l'ecriture, LA, Souffles,* and *Angst*—in contrast to the more properly novelistic works of half-closed narrative structures of plot development and intertextual binding: *Dedans, Le Troisième Corps, Commencements,* and *Neutre*—are self-surpassing, open-ended, flowing. Each of these texts generates from a juxtaposition to other writings. In fact, we wager that it is quasi-impossible to write a coherently explicative essay in narrative or structural terms about a process of their origins or "composition" in the ways that the texts of Samuel Beckett or the new novel have been scrutinized. There simply is no plausible, detectable matrix of form other than the matrix itself.

For Cixous, such a creation is a mother-born process by which the scriptor, in unity, finds a maternal drive within her, a force devoid of any and all oedipal mechanics; it is closer to an unconscious than the writing of the male because of the anatomical reasons Freud distinguished, much to the demise of the masculine cause, in his "Femininity," where the logic of argument demonstrates best what it tries to put in question.[52] Despite difference, the vagina, uterus, and pelvis contain both sexes.[53] The plenitude of feminist writing has a corporeal explanation so convincing, Cixous suggests, that all writers of force and passage are those giving birth to words flowing in accord with the contractual rhythms of labor.

For this reason, she always projects her text toward the sea. This is not just a facile play on words inherited from ninteenth-century lyrics confusing the mother with liquid and the ocean (*mer-mère*), but a drive to gravity emblematized in prose written in the shadow of Vermeer's paintings. Vermeer, she remembers, paints tableaux of women with an aura from the outside of the belly. The woman pouring milk pours radiance out of her room into the world to the left of the frame; the lady weighing gold reflects upon her pregnancy, giving cause to the golden hue of the space she occupies, and above her head infuses a painting of the Last Judgment with a new plenitude; she evokes the lacemaker who plays with the needle in order to parody the masculine instrument of "style" in the space of the tiny cadre.

For Cixous all this is the plenary will for the sea, the almost Proustian dilatation flowing toward the view of Delft from the double matrices of Illiers and the sun-splashed waters of Venice that can be recaptured whenever the woman writes out of the oedipal order and into the seaward channel. *Ver meer.* She uses the Dutch background to argue for the eruption of a rich unconscious surging, like light, from the privy parts of the female body:

> The vibrating flesh, the enchanted belly, the woman pregnant of all her love. No seduction, no absence, no gulf adorned with veils. Plenitude, that which does not look at itself, which does not reappropriate all its shapes reflecting from the face, never the eye-eater. She who looks with the look that recognizes, studies, respects, does not take, does not scratch, but attentively with a soft desire for flesh [*acharnement*] contemplates and reads, caresses, bathes, makes the other radiate. Brings back to life terrestrial life, fleeting, become too prudent. Illuminates it and sings its names.[54]

The text pleads that women begin writing with what they have, not—as a markedly psychoanalytical frame of reference would have it—from what the female lacks. Castration is to be found in neither her painterly source nor in any of the feminist writings. The pun in the name of Ver-meer (*vers-mer/mère*, toward the sea/mother) that allows this recovery makes the writing work all the easier.

In the same fashion, as we have seen, she emblematizes the breast not as a lack on which the male centers his glance, but rather on a pardoxically full concavity, an inner-breast inherited from the

German tongue of her mother; as she has it, it can be an all-inclusive *sein* heard in English as a primary *sign* and in French an adjective of health, a *sain*. The mother is revalorized not as a buxom object but as the one who both nourishes and gives birth. The female attribute is also, etymologically, at the origin of the fold of *sinus* which divides the sexes.

The woman writer, after separation from the mother, interiorizes her as a love object and will always, phantasmatically, find her in others and in texts she writes. The writer must re-traverse the mother as origin, voice, song, and body without killing her. She will write with the (absent) mother before the law and symbolization. Not the name of the mother. The young-born wonders: " 'And now what birth shall I give myself [*qui naître*: a play on *naître*, to be born, and *n'être*, not to be, in the sense of a constituted being]?' The voice of the mother says: 'I am here.' And all is here. If I had such a voice, I would not write, I would laugh. . . . I would not fear losing my breath [*essoufflement*]. I would not come to help myself with a text."[55] The breath of life, of voice gives birth to the text without any cut; the breath becomes writing. Each woman is triple: absent mother, mother/daughter, song and milk of the first voice that once touched her; *allaitement, halètement,* a play on feeding and breathing. Cixous invokes all the senses, touch, hearing, taste, no longer in hierarchical order. The mother—who is not a simple convention but maintains a link with flesh and blood—*is* the source of writing. The continuity of interiorization across time by means of love and procreation verifies the force of a *hysterical mystery* which is the stuff of a woman's discourse, complete and one to itself. The woman's writing therefore has its own presence, its own closure, impervious to the pointed desire of the man's appropriative or seductive discourse. Converse to the male, who at best can only *spray* his words, the writer-as-mother gives birth to and "nourishes" her text.

The entirely material condition in which the female must write and speak necessitates the use of discourse that gives words a negotiable value. Here is the crucial part of translation in Cixous's work in terms of both concept and style, and an "English" version of her work is always in danger of lacking the duplicity or undecidability of the words in French. Our argument would underscore Cixous's association of "mystery" and "hystery," the latter deriving from Joyce's nightmare of logocentrism; yet she attacks it visibly and audibly by virtue of hysteria. The musical mystery is shrill with screams and shrieks, assuring the passage of life flowing in accord with lunar cycles under the aegis of Diana and Natura. Cixous underlines the positive adventure of a nightmare, a nightmother, whose phantasms produce a flat writing detached from historical moorings. Only women can both feel and profess these rhythms coming into the world out of its own hollows: the uterus, seat of hysteria; the breast, which males figure falsely as plenitude; the loin and pelvis, whose rotund curves have the meanders of style and flow.

Rejoyce

In this light Cixous's profound affinities for Joyce are found, once again, in missexual writing, where the Irish novelist looked to a positive aspect of separation—not unlike the warm solitude of Vermeer's maidens. There the feminist language could write itself away from the overconceptual order and ever-mimetic drive of masculine letters. She admires the extreme musicalizing of words where, in *Finnegans Wake,* Joyce finally unstraps himself from representative shackles and infuses the written word with breath and rhythm.

Rythme is a portmanteau word intersecting the multiple features of the feminist enterprise. "Thus each text another body. But in each the same vibration: for what of me marks all my books and recalls that it is my flesh that signs them, it is a *rythme.* Medium my rhymed body, my writing."[56] Rhyme and reason are her self-imposed rite of writing. This *rite-me* convokes the female to find her nourishment in a festival of intensifications and in passage which, like a cure, traverses anguish and releases frustration by the vocative music of the printed word, accessible to the writer only when grammar and logic are used to repress the repressive influence so common to critical idiom.

In this mode Cixous ends her magistral *Exile of James Joyce.* Following Derrida's critique of the Platonic doctrine praising the spoken word, memory, and oral learning over the art (*technè*), remedy, and opinion of writing, and before embracing a feminist cause as such, she had insisted that Joyce dissociates himself from all forms of paternity, theology, and truth connected with the word. In Joyce, the dichotomy of Sham and Shaun, like that of speech and *écriture,* opens the dikes of a reservoir that had been under the capital control of the male. This uncanny connection between an Irish canon and Plato mark in Cixous the beginning of a feminist language to the degree that the irreconcilable oppositions in the text turn to derision the phallocratic order. Insofar as Shaun was proud of owning words and mastering men, he held "allegiance to capitalism and patriarchy" and was opposed to the innocuous double, Shem (or *sham(e)* of the *same* or the *seme*), who is "not an imitator but truly the inventor of a writing that does not seek to help or displace memory, but to live on its own perpetual contradiction, holding the reader always in attentive suspense."[57] It is here, in the eruption of force from the ancestral Pleiades up through the Dublin of Joyce and post-1968 Paris, that Cixous channels the energy for a program that was ever-incipient in her *oeuvre.*

Creatures from the Black Lagoon

Part of the difficulty a pragmatic feminism might encounter in Cixous's discourse would derive from the undecidability of the *sham,* which may be described as a dissimulating, duplicitous, amimetic concept that makes of writing a productively dead form assuring the woman of her life-giving language. Derrida had spoken of this as a new way by which we "must recognize writing in the spoken word, that is to say the difference and absence of the spoken word. There it is to begin thinking the lure."[58] Thinking of writing as *in no way* a reproduction of reality but as access to the more ma-

ternally primordial phantasm where contradictions do not exist—
that is the program catalyzed by the dummy, the artificial creature
(dis)simulating what had been held to be at once mimetic and au-
thentic. The ruse of the mannequin turns out to be a supremely
feminist ploy where writing fictionless fiction promotes the release
of semiotic energies which the male simply squanders in specular or
oedipal constraints, known as the product of the "mirror stage" or,
more generally, the "double bind" of schizophrenia. Hence, Cixous's texts always resemble novels written outside the Occidental
tradition. The tempo of their writing—indeed their lack of style—is
in cadence with lacunary moments of grammatical inconsistencies,
sentence fragments, image signs, portmanteau words, litanic inscriptions, and jets of letters of infinite regress. The novels in this
manner appear often nightmarish; *Angst,* for instance, is a long
dream-text of phantasmatic release *into* a glyphic world of letters.
By virtue of a writing that conveys the anguish, it permits the transgression of social taboo—here Sapphic joy. Lurid shapes, monsters
of the night of Goya's *caprichos,* the uncanny sandmen with eyes in
their pockets, prosthetic bodies manipulated by strings pulled by—
and independent of—the puppeteers above them: these are the
baby dolls transcribed to and from the real and in continual play
with that dimension. The movement between the creatures and
their autonomous mechanisms can be likened, as in Cixous's own
frequent analogies, to a neofeminist cure.

The Lure of the Text: LA

How the bionic woman throws herself into the *cielle, a* C-I-E-L-L-
E, into the empyrean where she will be a hear-she or sky queen, is
the subject of Cixous's writing in *LA.* One of the voices follows the
female flight that borders on a translinguistic reading cultivated by
many teachers of French: "She sets herself away from a dead-
male/moremale state [*elle s'écarte de l'état mortmâle*]. She climbs
up on her polygams [*ses polygames*]. She enraptures herself in al-
titude. She rapidly succeeds in an oral/auditive way in rising above

the buildings, the terraces with yards, the bell towers, all the suburban pretense. Through rich appetite: for the love of that which she could see if she succeeded in surmounting the edifices which prevent her from contemplating her infinite. Desire gives her the voice that carries her off."[59] Almost evoking a sense of dissillusionment to an intelligent reader by the facility of the image—the woman going to heights beyond herself, above the madding crowd that had been the stagnantly fecund earth out of which nineteenth-century poetics had grown—the text affixes itself to the paradox of a voice whose graphics conduct the body out of its entrails, over and above the vaguely defined masculine stricture of the *mortmâle* and the silence of an urban perspective figures by the cliché of the rooftops of Paris. Eating the spoken word with eyes that look toward the sun, the speaker discovers that she must mix her figures indiscriminately— even incestuously—in order to convey the phantasm of flight on the symbolic dimension of the page: in the context, she figures herself as a fish in a polluted pond who must look up to a bait on the horizon, covet it, jump up, swallow it, and realize the imaginary condition of the situation portraying it. Because of the resemblance of words to words, the lure in the Parisian scene is a penthouse apartment: "First one lets oneself be had. After the fact one looks for a reason everywhere. Where is the lure? The two- or three-room apartment has everything to repulse one. . . . To the line."[60] The upward thrust is impeded by the interference of a real, even practical, referent within the temptation of the *appât* (lure). Yet by letting the manifold dramas of apartments blend with those of fishing lures, the writer opts for an aesthetic that always borders on artifice.

The work forces a convergence of feminist criticism, philosophical writing, and the excess of fiction. The fabrication of a feminized *appât,* the simulacrum of text, has a collective function making the reader reconsider the perfection of copy. Cixous's text is both in and out of the mimetic system it embodies. Because of such indeterminacy, *LA* can best be situated next to the figures from which it emerges. Crucial is the way Cixous displaces seemingly unmarked concepts of modern criticism for her needs. To this end we shall use a middle section from Derrida's *Glas*, a text of neither patently feminist, meditative, nor literary stamp but whose process inseminates Cixous's fictional theory. The coextended comparison of *LA* with *Glas* will disengage a sense of what may be the most timely consequence of a feminized writing in the miss-concepted notion of a *missexual*. We must first determine how Cixous uses the woman Derrida withdraws from Hegel's *Phenomenology* and *Ethics*.

A Question of Ethics

Derrida meditates on the problem of the fetish in philosophy and literature. By retracing Hegel's discussion of the family and the central basis of *Sittlichkeit*, an ethics which must underpin all of Western culture, he opens a critical space in which a writer today—like the philosopher—is cornered: "Then contradiction springs up again: in its essentiality, singularity can only disappear; it can posit itself *as such* only in death. If then the family has a singularity for its proper object, it can only busy itself *around death*. Death is its essential object. It has for its destination the cult of the dead; it must consecrate itself to the organization of sepulture."[61] The critic disengages the difference between the family building itself on private enterprise, "in its right of possession and joy,"[62] and the government which must declare war against it. The state, as a virile crown, has to violate the woman (or family), reminding it that the master of all things is death and dissolution. The Hegelian solution to the war of the state and the family can only be one of intermittence, an intervalic rhythm of violence and harmony which Derrida will later erect in the figure of Dionysus in daily gymnastics. So, with the state and family or Apollo and Dionysus, "the absolute triumph of one over the other would lead to nothing. Every law is therefore a law of death,"[63] which is to work outside of a sepulchral monument between the binarities of life and death. The human laws of the state and its ancestors stand over the divine law of conservation; the woman must project herself into life-assuring roles beyond the often destructive and barbarous forces of the man. Where the male is associated with daylight, public virtue, and universality, and where he is conceptualized as the government of the city, the civil world, and the ideology of war, the female is nocturnal, natural, familial, and singular.

It follows from the reading of the *Ethics* that the result of the man's dutiful attack on the woman (or the state's necessary rape of the family for civic betterment) is the half-collective, half-individual volume of a plot in the cemetery. Bringing the cadaver back into her nocturnal matrix, as it is unconsciously figured, the woman must assure the reproduction and dramatic representation of death. The feminine process of mourning must impede the body from returning to its original state of nature. She embalms, buries, mummifies, and emplaces over the family a funeral stele through which the spirit will rise again. Hence death will never die. The new marriage of the body with the earth of the nation will hold in check the natural forces decomposing meaning from both within and without, from day and night. Hegel's heroine looms forth in Antigone, the woman who obstinately fought the state in defense of her brother's sepulture.[64] An erect figure of authority, Creon administers the familial laws that Antigone must combat. Her family is tragically pure: because the brother and sister are of chaste relation, and because their kinship is one of blood, like war, the messiness of incestuous desire is avoided. In the philosopher's argument, the subject of Sophocles' play becomes a *personnage* (character) divested of all features detrimental to a sound ethics. Raised higher than a mother, daughter, or spouse, yet feminine and seen in the "nature" of sexual difference, Antigone finds herself in a consanguine—not a uterine—family, which tempers the excesses of desire. Placed in a tomb, and dead before the onslaught of marriage, "she fixes herself, holds herself, benumbs and transfigures herself in this character of eternal sister carrying off with her womanly desire."[65] Enclosed in a self-willed womb, her mausoleum is the reassuring image of unity in Hegelian aesthetics: in his words, "the most admirable and most soothing work of art."

Exploiting Derrida's reading, Cixous will open this figure in *LA* in order to immerse life in Hegel's space of death. Wherever Hegel looks for the dream of calm, whether in Antigone or the separation of sentiment and duty, class preparation and conjugal bliss, there is always an "element excluded from the system which assures the space of possibility for the system"[66]—or, more simply rendered, the vomit, the supplement of the system needed to convey the system. Hegel, as Derrida suggests from the onset, is colossally, catachrestically figured by his own name: the HGL, an icy eagle (Hégel-Hegel-*aigle*) who must soar up and over its frozen state, then emulate the emblem of emblems, the eagle stamped by the world-historical personality of Napoleon, who rests in the tomb of the Invalides. To this, philosophy had to aspire and descend.

Any discussion of the tomb or petroglyph of the Hegelian system assuring its verticality informs the themes of a modern feminist stance less than it provides a model of the order against which it must be aimed, and with which the text has to function. In disclosing the limits of writing feminist tracts or novels "exclusive of" or "against" men, and by extension unveiling a generalized concern for the bodily life of language as does Derrida with Hegel, Cixous marks, delimits, and constrains an area where violence can be deployed effectively. There, sexual difference can be affirmed other than through opposition: in the syndrome of family and incest, in taboo which narrative has had to uncover and recover, she holds in an unceasing movement masculine and feminine, earth and sky, matrix and puncheon—all of which had been used to turn difference into opposition. Hers, like Derrida's, is a transcategorical and transsexual movement—which makes explication all the more difficult. She transgresses ethical limits by using limits that the practice of fiction and criticism prescribes. Yet the strength of the *concept* in her work—that which Hegel opposed to sentiment and feeling of a feminine realm, which historically had been one with a uterus giving birth to the novel—remains dominant, thanks to the intimacy with Derrida. And this is precisely her bait.

Some of the convergences in figures of "sepulture," stolen from

Glas for different use in the mode of fiction, put the conceptual side of the novel and its transmission to the text. *LA* begins with the "Book of the Dead Ladies," a volume designating the abysmal space out of which the woman writer will come.

Who during the weighing of words will spring forth from my mouth? Animated, pressed, what a crowd, precisely after a first death, inhabits my depopulated regions. Hazy, gay but nobody! Is part of my following. Who is dreaming? I am at my sides, at the same time upstairs in the gallery when in the city which I plunged into mourning, my new brother tears away from my enemies my left arm, the arm of the Orient which they have stolen from me in my absence.

Oh my former bodies, my breaths, my days of the past! where, now, who accompanies me, whom to accompany?[67]

As if designating the tomb of an unknown soldier from which her voice must flow to find adequate accompaniment of other songs and other bodies, the speaker begins where Hegelian ethics ended: above and below herself, on the verge of spewing out of herself. She strikes a meticulously drawn cliché of the lyrical novel so evident in the passage just cited. Cixous mimes the dutiful Antigone, but without the sanction of purity that had given splendor to the Hegelian heroine. By the indistinction of referents, the voice is also that of a chimera, a who-mother and benevolent monster who will establish a space of betweenness or marginality without any of the sexual trappings of night and day, family and country, which had beset Hegel's fetish of the ideal woman. In the formless opening and closing of *LA,* Cixous affirms a sense of independent, almost "newborn" and "young-born" life which must use the concept of the mausoleum for its point of vertical and horizontal departure.

The text calls for those who will accompany it outside of its present condition, before and after writing; chants, songs, and dreams are evoked to give a collective resurgence of fiction; the melody effaces any and all sign of the unilateral author, primal force, Natura, or nocturnal muse. It may well be at its fortuitous end that *LA* steps into the space of the Hegelian erection in order to lure masculine/conceptual and feminine/lyrical voices of writing from the historical process that had excluded the lack of either or both. So the Invalides must look to the Eiffel Tower:

> It is without problem that a minute later I land in a square, an island of safe territory.
>
> But of the descent from the first stories, there remains bitterness. There was a lack of bliss, but that is not serious. . . . No, no, my art is perfect. I am even ready to start again, in an instant. I raise my head. Up there, pink and veiled above the urban cubes of mediocre height, rises the Effelle tower. It is from there that we must throw ourselves. Then, no dimension would be lacking. To make fun of threats, without wings [*ailes*] get away from the pole, without anguish, with them [*elles*], to pass with one's souls, one's forms, and all one's letters to the infinite where she will tune into her *la*.[68]

An impersonal, nameless Eiffel Tower replaces the antique pyramid and its mummies. As the eyes of the narrator climb the fleshy girding of the urban stele, the body is ready to jump away—from there, from the letter of *la* with the chants and notes of other women (*sans ailes, avec elles*): but the female *là*—with an *accent grave*—is and is not a toponym indicated by an index finger pointing in the direction of its own inscription in the rosy veil of the *FL* tower, no longer one of the aquiline majesty of a Hegelian aesthetic, a signature of HGL, but an *effel*, discreetly spelling out its orthographic difference from both the architect of modern philosophy and the initials of the woman's liberation movement. And the flying form of her tower, we have seen, is in part a derivative of the double *f* emblazoning the *féminin futur* begun in *La Jeune Née:* "It is from there that we must throw ourselves by traversing the skyline of Paris with letters in a takeoff of infinity, where the *elle* (*L*) will resonate."[69] Cixous remodels the fragmented crescents of Mallarmean fingernails scratching up and above to dedicate and unspeak their onyx, an interferent that cannot be dissociated from the reading, yet which she elicits in an excessive, pansexual force of birth overflowing narrow dialectical boundaries.

The enterprise may appear chimerical, and the synthesis in the distance from Hegel difficult to ascertain. Conflating sexual opposition into the missexual voice of *LA,* Cixous writes formlessly, without respect for the binaries that allow anlaysis to take place. In attempting to project herself like herself, Cixous uses the lure Derrida puts on the edge of his discourse on Hegel. Derrida expands the notion of *prosthesis* at the end of thesis and antithesis. In Cixous, the figure of a *jeune née* jumping from the *effelle* tower is born artificially. In Derrida's words, "Hegelian dialectic, mother of criticism, is first of all, like every mother, a daughter."[70] Hence the formless form of an embryonic writing jumping in and out of its phantasms must become the arabesque festooning the column of philosphy, the tracing of the future feminist *style.*

The missexual drive of separation from a matrix locates the moment of "crossing over," trance, or scandal in modern criticism. In and out of this fictional volume, the modern writer must pass to devaluate figures of speech cultivated by the neo-Hegelian authority that dictates many current trends of taste.

In *Angst,* Cixous writes the anguish of paradoxical rapture toward another body in what a proto-Hegelian public would deem perverse:

> During a catnap, you go out. A dream persuades you that you are not outside, you sleep, you are in your bed [*tu n'es pas dehors, tu dors, tu es dans ton lit*]. It's a shadow chinesing you in the street. Who runs in prancing, half rat, half me, blacker than you, and the streets in returning wind it up, as the belly is small, we believe we walk forward for eternity, we run with eyes shining in the dark, it smells of blood, suddenly the end, it smells of pussy, the snout opens. Already! What an awakening! Ripped with the most extreme violence away from nonbeing, from unconsciousness, brought back to itself by the occasion of the worst! An hour without claws, but all teeth outside.[71]

Couched in monologue of dialogue, where the voice reconstructs in a dream the dialectics of love, the text generates waves of force through its departure from a Hegelian form—thanks to the phantasm breaking down the difference between outside and inside, *de-*

dans and *dehors*. The absent interlocutor is not outside; she sleeps in the valley of text, a bed or surface of letters, awakening from the nightmare of cats scratching the flesh in the pain of a prelude to love. The characters (persons as letters) turn into felines. *TOUTES DENTS DEHORS:* teeth, talons, and philosophical position conflate in the audible shape—da. The phantasm can only be so with music and letters, phonics and graphics. Hence the "shadow chinesing you in the street," a material lettered dream that all of a sudden opens for the reader a grammarless program of errant reading: the shadow which *te chinoise* in the theater of cat and rat, in silhouette ceding to the visible analogue; "on croit *cheminer* pour l'éternité," where the emerging che- or *chi* (X) makes the meeting of two characters both dream and possibility, of which the text itself is a "preparation for detachment," a cat (*chat*) crossing all the prefixes (chi-che-cha), whose object is skinned alive: *rappelé* (called back) or *rat pelé* (a skinned rat).

Angst writes both a detachment and an arrival. Written out of anguish, in anguish, it moves away from a masculine writing scene toward a feminine one: "There is a woman, the Living, the spirit of life knowing itself and wanting itself, while I was losing my body in anguish, a woman set on asserting life, decisive, a Thought without model. . . . She the most solitary for having made possible the locus, beyond the restricted economy of death, where stretches and spends itself without limits the love that knows how to give outside of the trajectory of castration."[72] There, another writing, conjoining body and thought, will be.

4

Accord Koré to Cordelia

"Des Femmes"

Having reached an intellectual limit, Cixous ascertains that she could displace it only by turning from the inscription of difference in a heterosexual (even bisexual) to a homosexual scene. The meeting at the crossing of text and biography of a living woman and the (dead) Brazilian writer Clarice Lispector coincides with a temporary change in publishers, from the established houses of Grasset, Denoël, and Gallimard to the controversial "Des Femmes" (women, of women, belonging to women), a gesture that Cixous considers as a political act.

The Dionysian affirmations, the Joycean missexual puns beyond metaphysical oppositions, are now displaced—in her ongoing search for a rewriting of sexual *differance and* a new affective economy—toward a play between masculine and feminine but in such a way that feminine tends to come back to woman. The "homosexual scene" between quotation marks, without model and law, functions very differently from the lesbian one, which reproduces for Cixous a masculine, phallocentric structure. Because of their cultural position *and* their life-giving function, women are more open to a homosexuality that writes itself in a play of voices, where an open container and contained infinitely flow into each other.

Poetically Political, Politically Poetic

Poetically political, politically poetic—the chiasmatic aphorism traverses Cixous's writing from *Vivre l'orange* to *Limonade tout était si infini*. The poetic aspect is not mere ornament but—as Roman Jakobson has shown in his analysis of the six functions of verbal communication—the function in which the message takes itself as object, is not linked to a referent, and gives the reader the sensation of something beautiful. This self-love of the signifier is accompanied by a graphic, phonic, material aspect and prevents any dichotomy of the sign. In Cixous, the poetic functions both aesthetically *and* strategically. Its aim is to undo a homogeneous, dominant discourse that hides its will to power beneath eternal, conceptual truths. Poetry is not opposed to politics; it is more political than a so-called political discourse, itself already part of another system.

At the summit (what used to be called fiction): poetry and the poet. The poet-writer has uncanny resemblance to the one on whom Derrida meditates in "Economimesis."[1] For Kant, writes Derrida, the beautiful is that which derives from a nature which produces. The artist's freedom resembles God's through nonimitation. The passage of mimesis must not proceed by concept but by almost natural productions which will institute the nonconceptual rules of art. The poet is superior to the conceptual orator. He gives more for less. He announces a simple play of the imagination, but by playing, he gives nourishment to the understanding (*entendement*) and life to the concept. The poet escapes the contract (debt and recognition); his overabundance generously interrupts a circular economy. The poet has recourse to voice. Poetry is the least imitative of the arts. Cixous feminizes the major terms and inserts them in a slightly different chain: productive nature, poet, voice, gift (*don*). In Derrida's reading of Kant, the poet transmits the poetic gift and allows this *plus value* to go back to an infinite source that can never be lost. This opens onto circulation, to giving and receiving, to investing and spending. Thus, as soon as the infinite gives itself to thinking, the opposition between restricted and general economy, between circulation and productivity of spending, is erased. It is even, if one may still say so, the *function* of the passage to the infinite: the passage *of* the infinite between gift and debt.[2]

Cixous writes (from) this return to the infinite source, (from) a passage *to*—rather than *of*—the infinite. Erasing the first term of the Kantian analogical schema that determines laws:

God   nature
↓   ↓
nature   human genius

she generalizes and rewrites the second:

(nature)–(absent) mother
↓
poet-mother-daughter

In Kant, the relation between analogies is always of language, a language linked to the senses, especially to those that nourish (mouth, ear), which will spill over (*déborder*) contractual limits. Cixous's chain gets longer: source, mother, poet, plenitude; the divine resonances of a hierarchical value scale are never quite absent. Classifying the senses, Kant had distinguished between the mechanical senses of hearing, sight, and touch and the chemical senses of taste and smell. The former are linked to perception, the latter to pleasure (*jouissance*). There are qualitative differences between the two groups as well: smell and taste, as *jouissance,* rank higher than sight and touch, which are completely exterior. Though for Kant pleasure and knowledge, taste and knowledge, are dissociated, he admits that "in times immemorial" pleasure had commanded knowledge as experience, preceding the gap between *jouir* (to have pleasure) and knowing. For Cixous, women-as-beings-of-proximity are still back in, or must go back to, "those times" when knowledge is, was, not predicated on distance and sight but has the immediacy of smell, taste, and touch.

In the same essay, Derrida writes about the economy of a desire in relation to negative pleasure:

I take off from the negative. Kant admits the possibility and the concept of *negative pleasure.* For example, the feeling of the sublime. While "from the beautiful is born directly a feeling of intensification of life, to which can be joined the attractions and the play of the imagination, this [the feeling of the sublime] is a pleasure which springs forth (*entspringt*) only indirectly, that is to say, in such a way that it is produced by the feeling of an instant inhibition (*Hemmung:* of an arrest, a retention) of vital forces followed right away by a discharge (*Ergiessung:* overflow) all the stronger of the same forces [the corporeal schema here, since there is *Wohlgefallen*, pleasure, is that of ejaculation rather than of vomit, which this overflow could at first resemble]. It is an emotion, continues Kant, which seems to have nothing to do with play but consists in a serious occupation of the imagination. It cannot be reconciled with attraction; the mind being not only attracted by the object but, inversely, always again repulsed, the *Wohlgefallen* of the sublime contains less a positive pleasure than admiration or respect; that is to say, it deserves to be called negative pleasure.[3]

From Derrida's reading sexualizing Kant's textual economies, via Jean-François Lyotard's *Economie libidinale,* Cixous derives her own theory of libidinal economies, the effects of which she attempts to read in artistic texts. She distinguishes between two economies, one *masculine* (as exemplified by Kant's quote and Derrida's comment above): centralized, short, reappropriating, cutting, an alternation of attraction-repulsion; one *feminine:* continuous, overabundant, overflowing. These economies produce differences in inscription on the textual level, but they do not refer to one or the other of the sexes in exclusive fashion. They are, at all times, to be found in varying degrees in *both* men and women. Yet because of cultural repressions, an economy said to be feminine may more often be found in women. In spite of quotation marks and the insistence on displacing terms, a certain circularity is established, and there is always the possibility of an equation between feminine and woman, an equation on which Cixous herself seems to play, perhaps for political reasons. In what then would be a simple reversal, women—because of their relation to spending—would be superior to, better than, men. To speak of women as "more . . . than" without mentioning the other term in the comparison is not a blind spot in the theory but rather a point of uneasiness that threatens to reverse the two economies (and why only two?) into a hierarchical plus and minus. The praise of women (*des femmes*) as women is particularly insistent during Cixous's association with Des Femmes.

As a poet, Cixous does not develop a system, a philosophy of language. Yet language is all-important in her continuous rewriting of sexual *differance*. It is commonplace to say that language kills, that the word always implies the absence of the other. The play of absence-presence then is a political question. To proceed, to write, poetically, politically, one must approach the other slowly with words that do not kill or incorporate. One must remain other and alive. Such a poetic writing stresses the importance of the living, of a different affective economy; it goes against such notions as thetic moments or mirror stages, against all that cuts, divides.

The strategy now consists in advancing questions by working on specific textual problems with consequences in the "real." To be exorbitant, to write a *sortie,* Cixous's texts must remain questions of method rather than give univocal answers that would name and close the circuit. She does not propose the ready-made recipe, to be used and applied. In time, some questions—like that of Dora, of hysteria—become closed and must be left behind for others. Each text explicitly raises a question which is then written out poetically. Among the most important are those dealing with circulation of property: who is being circulated? how does circulation take place? In language, the question is related to naming: what is it to call a name? a name of a woman? This in turn evokes another: who writes? who is written? Or: who waits? how does one wait? Each text weaves the questions through a reading of other texts: Lispector, Kafka, Rilke, Virgil, Dostoevski, Shakespeare, and so on. Less conspicuously experimental, the poetry of these texts often resides in their phonic, musical quality. Some of them are available as cassettes; voice is that which gives them life, a voice which, for Cixous, has a corporeal origin and comes from far before a divided, enunciating "I." This voice breathes, sings, and then is suddenly translated to the page, to writing.

As a constant in all of her work, Cixous insists on displacing *séparation,* based on metaphoric death, with *réparation* and healing. This sets her apart from the main trend, emphasizing death, in contemporary letters. In a constant affirmation of life, Cixous tirelessly rewrites the same scene but in constant displacement. From Bataille and Hegel, the problematic of exchange and gift shifts, in congruence with other literary and critical trends, to the problem of the addressee, of *schicken* and *schenken*—sending and giving—as well as of receiving. From *Prénoms de personne,* from the shattering of the subject, the equivocal Olympia as doll or real, Morella as the presence of an absence, Cixous shifts to *prénoms de présence* (first names of presence).[4] Writing comes to involve the *presque,* the imperceptible, the minute. For Cixous, there is a sublime which is infinitely small and that will in any case remain incomprehensible and enigmatic. To privilege the small rather than the colossal displaces the limits not only between men and women but also between human beings and animals, human beings and plants.

Cixous calls the other in such a way as to leave as much life and presence of the other as possible: "While I was talking about presence, she went by, I did not forget her. A distance formed—it is not a separation. Written caresses survive in the sense of a triumph of life."[5] However, "to write *of*" always slips into "to write *on,*" which puts the writing subject in a position of mastery. Cixous wants to write as much as possible *of* or *with* a body, a thing, that exists in an instant never arrested, fixed, but leading to the next instant of presence, essence. Not the tomb, the mummification. The other remains distant in her proximity, forever other, not to be appropriated, repressed, forgotten. Women are more open to otherness because of their cultural position and because of their relation to the child, a relation thought of as the effect of *jouissance,* of pleasure, rather than on the level of the organ. They know how to *s'eautrer* (to become other in birth water) as *mer-mère* (sea-mother) and to communicate preverbally from unconscious to unconscious. To write *with,* derived from the English expression *to be with child,* insists less on a presence, a perception, than on a *process* of gestation and birth, away from an irreversible genealogy, there where the word "thank you" is tuned into birth music. The woman poet (in maternal plenitude) writes from where there is almost no law, guilt, contract, separation. Women poets, this time sexually marked, are more open to this kind of writing than men because of their relation to the child. Men's relation to the other is always one of exteriority. It is based on absence, death; women's on presence, life. This Cixous writes out in her texts, theorizes in her readings.

In a recent seminar at Paris VIII, she read the effects of these different economies in Rilke and Lispector. In Rilke's poem to Eurydice she disengages what she calls the classic masculine structure of the poet who calls his (absent) beloved and makes her even more absent through the literal dispersion of her name: E, I.[6] Eurydice dismembered is behind Orpheus. Always already lost, she *is* at the locus of separation without possibility for reparation. Melancholia, mourning, detachment are masculine attributes. Women as life-givers stress the continuum. Masculine effects are inscribed as cutting, fragmenting; the feminine ones are duration, continuity, breadth.

In contrast to Rilke's blissful mourning, Lispector's somatic writing approaches the other peacefully, patiently, innocently.[7] Language is thought from the living, not from an alienating mirror stage; Lispector teaches how to approach things: she gathers. The allusion is to Heidegger's meditations on reading as both *lesen* (to read) and *Lese* (harvest, gathering). Reading, far from being a simple act of glancing at letters, at pages, is in fact a gathering, a harvest. The French *cueillir,* to gather, to pick, also plays on *se recueillir,* to meditate. "Clarice lets (be)," notes Cixous; the gift takes place. This is what she calls a feminine answer to Derrida's reading of a gift which, linked to time, never really takes place for the philosopher. The response is not worked through Derrida's (unpublished) text but simply sent from Cixous's feminine, poetic border. At the summit the poetic, the feminine, freed from theoretical subjugations; below, the philosophical, the masculine, which can only ruse with the system. "The voice Clarice picks. And tends us the orange. Gives us back the thing. That which the orange says precisely at the call of its voice, its juice of the moon, gives it to us to drink."[8] The word is not quite the thing, nor does it replace the thing. The gift is less a violent *dépense* of passion and destruction, of explosions and coincidence beyond opposites, than a giving-receiving in slow approach, in a language of the imperceptible, so minute that the word, always linked to time, to a *cheminement*, is *almost* the thing. This is where the gift is possible, where giving and receiving are almost simultaneous and constantly engender each other, the way two women or twin sisters engender each other. If to receive is a science, to know how to receive is a gift. A new affective economy changes the relationship to one's body, to that of the other: an economy of the gift through love. Yet this economy, said to be feminine, is not reserved to women alone. Scenes from Kleist are reread away from slashing Z's and lightning, from the letter F as ubiquitous phallus, toward a (violent) movement of love, toward the other: it is a question of a gift of love for Toni in *The Fiancés of San Domingo,* for Käthchen von Heilbronn, Michael Kohlhaas, even for Penthesilea.

These differences in libidinal economies subtend, structure, and organize writing. Reverting to a (culturally) nominal distinction, Cixous writes that men have written nothing but cases (*boîtes*)[9]— or kases, the harsh sound of the letter K being for her the masculine letter par excellence[10]—structures governed by the law, pyramidal constructions containing death. Women on the other hand are writing out of the frame, out of the case. Unlike Kafka's K., they are not content to wait before the law. Therefore, they become themselves cases for society and cannot be forgiven (*pardonnées*)—from Dora (a case of hysteria) to Cixous, whose right to grant credit for her seminar was temporarily revoked by government officials in 1980. Women write out of the frame, in tune with their bodies. Their works have different (bodily) rhythms. Each text, each question will have a different format. One need only look at the visual impact of Cixous's texts of the past few years: alternating typefaces, the omission of paragraphs, white spaces. These are more than mere technical aspects of experimental writing; they convey this overflow.

During her association with Des Femmes, though critical of separatism, Cixous did in fact polarize men and women. True, the criticism is leveled against phallocrats (men *and* women), but the rather general use of the terms "men" and "women" reinforces a hierarchical reversal. In a period of transformation, the generalization of the negative term, women, may be necessary, but she cannot arrest it, make it into a master *concept*. Singing and praising women as giving, Cixous does not, unlike other feminists, address and decry men as retaining, except in textual readings. This is part of her mobile strategy that wants to displace difference into *différance* but without acceding to a beyond that would be a new synthesis. In Cixous's "homosexual" scene, the heavily sedimented term has to be read with caution. Writing from woman to woman, from *elle,* does not in itself draw a separatist line between men and women. It simply proposes a structure without law, model, or separation.

This structure, to repeat, is intimately linked to a return to the origin, to the mother-as-source. Cixous insists on a source of voice as both interior and exterior. The source is the voice of the other, a written voice that traces, spaces, writes. From then on, every woman is triple: as mother, daughter, and absent mother. The matrix of fiction is that engendering of a sister by her twin sister. But insofar as writing as inscription is to some degree a phallic activity and as everyone has two parents, writing always depends on both father and mother. A woman writer must be legitimized by her father as stylus and the mother as *écriture.* A woman's writing will depend in part on her relationship to her (imaginary) father and mother. While some women, like Virginia Woolf, have denied the father and identified with the mother, others, like Simone de Beauvoir, have identified with the father and rejected the mother. Still others, like Cixous herself, have been legitimized by the absent (dead) father *and* by the mother.

A Return to the Origin: Vivre l'orange

Vivre l'orange: to live (the) orange, to live the fruit and the color, a displacement of the former "I see orange" from *Portrait du Soleil.*

To live the fruit, the flower would transform one's relation to words, things, others. Orange would be beyond the old binaries of masculine and feminine. Colors would replace the fatality of the one, two, of the pair. "D'Oran-je," Cixous had written in *Portrait du Soleil*, linking her North African origin to a sanguine orange. *Vivre l'orange* returns to the same fruit. A comparison of the "titles" marks the distance between the two texts. Read across Bataille, Freud's Dora, Lacan, and Derrida, *Portrait* dealt with displacements of negative aspects of separation in relation to (the eye of) the law. In *Portrait*, Cixous wrote of a violence that would not be reversible into a plus, a minus, a victor or vanquished, one that would undo meaning in a violent coincidence beyond opposites. *Vivre l'orange* emphasizes the living proximity of the wor(l)d via ear, touch, smell, taste—continuity rather than fragmentation. The orange is less a simulacrum of the sun, god, father, capital than a present in the world. The wor(l)d *is* fruit, felt and tasted.

Cixous reintroduces some "concepts" she had earlier discarded: being, presence, essence are terms she uses between quotation marks—signaling the possibility of iteration—rather than ontologically. From a ruseful, artificial writing of the lure, of nonpresence, nonorigin, Cixous turns toward a matrical writing of prenature, prelaw, before the erection of a nature-culture division, to a vegetal, earthen (yet "culturally" natural) writing: "the great writing, the writing of other days, the terrestrial vegetal writing, of the time when the earth was the sovereign mother, the good mistress, and we went to the school of growth in her countries."[11] "Sovereign" functions as an attribute of the mother, a kind of Roman Domina, and no longer as that of a coincidence of opposites. Unlike Francis Ponge—for whom objects lose their familiar, everyday status and become uncanny, menacing, and anguishing—Cixous advocates a writing in which objects become familiar yet remain mysterious, strange.

In *Portrait*, Cixous had written about the orange: "The first time I cut a word it was it."[12] In *Vivre l'orange* the fruit is not cut as in *Portrait du soleil*. Life-giving, whole, it opens to general circulation and not only to that prescribed by the law. There, the woman writer sings in bliss and pathos. The orange appeals to (*appelle,* calls) all senses by correspondence, a term with echoes from Rimbaud's and Baudelaire's poems and epistolary exchanges past and present. The emptying of the self, the movement toward and from the source without self, opens to a paradoxical art of innocence, of the insignificant. The detailed, material writing where naming does not precede but advances toward the other and keeps alive—this is what she now calls an art of the sublime without sublimation. It is a nonincorporating approach in an economy of love, in the quivering instant where the gift takes place.

Cixous writes from her poetic freedom of essence (perfumes, taste), presence (to let the thing be), at the confines of alterity or there where alterity is the essence of the "other" reality. Writing poetically, she can disregard the constraints of theory. She infuses her texts with theory but without enclosing herself in what she calls "its limits." In *Vivre l'orange,* Clarice Lispector becomes Cixous's engendering source, the orange to be tasted in innocence in a quasi-simultaneous movement of giving and receiving, of reading and writing:

Clarice is entirely in the instant when she gives herself to being alive, infinite, unlimited in her being. When I say Clarice, it is not simply to speak to you and of a person; it is to call Clarice a joy, a fear—a frightened joy. To give you this joy, to give you this fear, this joy in a fear.

—To know who is the joy, where, to know her non-face, her features strikingly mobile, almost immobile. Fear of joy?

To have the fortune—little sister of joy—to have encountered the joy clarice, or the joy *g h* or *l* or anna, and since then to live *in* joy, in her infinitely great arms, her cosmic arms, dry and warm, tender, slim—The too great fortune?—[13]

The voices of women flow into one another, celebrate one another. Flower women, women as flowers, clarice, begonia, rose, in lower key let flowers open: "There is a way of saying tulip which kills every tulip. There is a clarice-way of making tulip from the stem to the sloe [*prunelle:* in French a play on sloe, pupil and *apple* of the eye], I see like the tulip is true."[14]

Returning to the garden metaphor of one of her first texts, *Un Vrai Jardin,* Cixous writes: "To inhabit was the most natural joy when I was still living inside; all was garden and I had not lost the way in."[15] She searches for a paradise garden before the Fall, which would not be the paradoxical space of *Dedans* but one where she could live "in the intimate outside."[16] The tone is less one of nostalgia, melancholia, and mourning than one of active search to repair the loss. Words separate. Women have been cut off from the bodily source, from the mother who heals. The unspoken accusation is against the phallocentric society with its hard affective economy: "But in these feeble times and forgetful times, when we are far away from things, so far from each other, very far from ourselves, in these sad and forgetful times, of feeble looks, too short, falling aside from things, far from living things, where we do not know how to read, to let sense radiate, and we are cold, a glacial air is blowing around our souls, around the words, around the moments, our ears are frozen, the years have four winters and our ears hibernate, we have need of translation."[17] Instead of *traduction,* translation, Cixous proposes *translation*—a difference lost in English—by correspondence, vibrations in an infinitely expansive tissue. Her approach to Lispector is not unlike that which Heidegger had advocated in his readings of Friedrich Hölderlin.[18] To let the other be as other, one has to call her so as to let her resonate, rather than to name and kill her. Similarly, a text cannot be read to gain knowledge and accrue power; it must be felt and make the reader vibrate. This is what Cixous calls "a *matter* of life and death."

Still haunted by the law which, for her, is nothing but a *word,* she urges women to turn away from maps of culpability (*les cartes de culpabilité*), from a language after the Fall. The poet has to "self-strange herself" to the point of absolute innocence, one not reversible into guilt. She must let herself be carried in front of thought, into the thought in preparation, the way Hölderlin had been called by ancient silence and had retired in prenatal Greece to give his life to nature. Traversing the map of innocence where strange names are calling them, women must hollow out a silence to the bottom and forget, in time, a space for the instant of a rose.[19] Cixous tries to make the word approach the thing as much as possible without falling back into a simple substantialism. The essence of the other remains the other essence which empties, estranges the self. The "self" addresses an other, but not an absent other. The poet must rethink her writing activities in such a way as to *désoublier* (to unforget), *détaire* (to unsilence), *déterrer* (to unbury), *se désaveugler* (to unblind), *se dessourdir* (to undeafen), in an endeavor to displace all that has been repressed, incorporated, appropriated. This is the poet's way of fighting.

To call (the Name of) a Woman: Illa

Illa raises the question of separation; of sending, giving, receiving; of investing and disinvesting in relation to writing and the Orphic myth—the equivalent in letters of the oedipal myth in psychoanalysis. Who sings? Who makes the poet sing? Who is being sung? Who is called or recalled? To whom does the poet write? Who is present, who is absent? Most writing under the sign of castration has been done in the Orphic mode. Orpheus sings the dead Eurydice. Orpheus advances, and Eurydice follows at his back. Man leads, woman follows toward daylight, clarity, reason, self-consciousness. The model itself is quite limited to one position, one (linear) direction. The way the poet advances functions as a metaphor for the poetic process, and the political consequences of the positioning of the bodies are undeniable. Eurydice is sung but lost, dead, absent.

Cixous proposes the myth of Demeter, goddess of the earth, of fecundity, who at the same time *is* the earth and roams the earth in search of her daughter Koré. Cixous changes the Greek name Persephone, which had been used by male theoreticians to allude to problems of voice (*phonè*), to the more material Koré (*corps-ai*), substituting the masculine letter K for the more commonly used C.

Demeter finds her daughter *alive* in an underworld that she also contains. Demeter is not limited to a narrow linear passageway. She traverses and contains unlimited spaces of world, sea, and underworld. Mother and daughter flow into each other as container and contained.[20] They sing to a pastoral tune of reparation rather than to an Orphic tune of separation. Most poetic myths are concerned with (re)calling another. The name (of a woman) that is being called functions as a substitute for the person. Writing is necessarily based on a certain absence, the solitude of the writer, and the permanence of the written trace but always to a matter of degree.

Illa, that one, he-she—with resonances from Heidegger's *il y a, es gibt,* there is—displaces the Orphic myth predicated on sight and the death of woman. Instead of Orphic separation and rewriting Derrida's *il y a cent blancs,* she proposes a language of reparation where the gift takes place, a maternal language with effects on metaphor, translation, debt, social contract.

Illa "begins" with a search for writing, with a voice questioning: "Who? Am I? Whom do I follow? The third one. Runs on the borderline of the earth, of the sea. Who(s)? am I, are we? Who I? We? Errs outside of she. Illa. A young person. The third one. In the middle of a double absence of peace. *Illa:* 'Quis et me' inquit 'miseram et te perdidit, o tu, quis tantus furor?' [Who both thee and me hath ruined and made wretched, what dreadful madness?]"[21] The third one escapes binary structures and their implicit possibilities of reversal. Simultaneously herself and outside of herself, *er* (he) outside of she, she runs along limits on her *sandales ailées* (winged sandals), not on the same shore but on sutures between earth-mother and sea-mother. A young *personne,* a person and nobody, whose name does not classify, arrest. The classic Orphic myth is displaced by a quote from Virgil's pastoral *Book of Farmers* (IV, i) in which Eurydice accusingly points to a structure that had made both male and female miserable. Woman searches for writing:

Who? Is hurrying? In steps like those of a white she-wolf. A long hand, long fingers, tireless, nervous, attentive, listens, acute, notes at length, is not a hand that takes note, is she's, a woman, here she is partridge, surrounded by little ones, gathers her trembling fingers, the whole body up to the wrists, makes she's, in the step of five, from birds, here she is panther, crouched, is but a jump, poignant, ready, kept back in the palm, in the back, the fingers galvanized. A noble hand. Long strides. She-camel which rises from the desert. A writing. Ankles like needles.

The third one does not say anything.[22]

An English translation can only treacherously render the rhythmic vibrations, the long even sounds of the French: "*A pas de louve blanche. Une main longue, longs doigts inlassables, nerveux.*" The extreme musicalization conveys the search for a meditative writing, not from the step beyond the crossed blades of X, but in long, slow steps of *cheminement,* with hands searching, hands stretched out from women to women. She who notes is never alone, in solitude but always *with* she's who dictate.

Writing always "begins" with an absence, a withdrawal of felicity, as coming into the world implies a necessary exteriorization. Each woman is triple from then on: daughter, mother, and absent mother. Coming to writing is a search for a *langue maternelle,* a maternal tongue of touch and taste (different from a *discours d'elle* or *de L* from *Glas*), a language that searches for and comes from the other(-mother). How does the poet call (the name of) a woman? A question Derrida had asked from a masculine border through readings of Blanchot's texts. *Illa* searches for the voice of the (absent) mother: "Called? Hears voices, her voices. Her voice. All the voices that breathe between languages and memories. Pre-hears. Does not see two feet in front of her body. Weak eyes. To hear. The look listens, listens."[23] Bodily vibrations, rhythms, and their translations into voice (and script) are heard with the ear of the other or another ear. The eye hears. The voice enters the ear as it envelops the person. *Listen, listen* forever doubles the sounds which resonate endlessly. "*Daurades dormeuses d'eaux profondes* [golden fish sleepily gliding through deep waters]. Blind and assured navigation. Slides in between two waters. The third one in her other waters."[24] The golden fish women reminiscent of Dora—whose name is dispersed in *daura, dor, d'eau*—reflect their own light in darkness. Not content with pushing *back* (a play on *dos* as back and musical notation in the dispersion of do's in the text), with deferring philosophical limits, women swimmers glide through waters, spaces without closures. They do not depend on the sun as god-father-capital; they escape the econommimetic bind. The deadly sirens of yesteryear have been replaced by the serene swimmers. Letters touch and caress. Voices are breaths of life, and they are never completely detachable nor detached from the bodies, as Derrida would argue. Discontinuities are but discreet interruptions, immediately followed by reparation. Weak eyes do not apprehend through sight, do not witness debt. Sound weaves a continuous thread that is never cut. The O's no longer encircle the absences they contain, they are open, round letters of plenitude, in a language that comes back to a selfless open self.

Mother and daughter. Demeter and Koré. Demeter both traverses the earth and is the earth. As mother, she never cuts the thread, does not know separation, detachment. Mother and daughter (*fille d'elle*, daughter of her, *fille d'aile*, a winged daughter with allusions to the female genitals, and *fidèle*, faithful) do not betray each other; they infinitely exchange and pass into each other without cutting. The thread (*fil*) that links mother, daughter, and sister is continuous, unlike that of the father-son (fils) relation, where the convention of filiation was based on naming and on killing the father. Women make up a *ronde*—in a movement neither linear nor ascending—such that "container" and "contained" ceaselessly flow into each other. *Ronde* evokes dancing, a musical step, as well as a note, a vigil, a patrol (*faire la ronde*), writing, a round hand; it displaces to some degree the more masculine *post*, both ma(i)le and post, with resonances of *ça tombe* (it falls) and castration. Women keep watch but while holding hands and touching. Demeter's round uterus remains open; it does not imprison; it feels the other in a life-giving gesture before the distancing effects of sight. Women are closer to the somatic, the pulsional, to a preverbal language based on rhythm and vibration, felt from the inside or heard through the ear. Cixous does not elaborate on the relationship between writing (and its necessary part of repression), music, tact, and the mixture of Dionysian and Apollonian elements. Though for her the origin of writing lies in music rather than in the image, *rhythm* remains a floating term. She ascertains a ductility of vibrations from unconscious to unconscious, drives that articulate the unconscious and are translated to the page as writing. In the women's *ronde,* dancers hold each other by the hand, *mains tenant, maintenant* (holding hands, now), in a moving present and presence, dancing to a pastoral tune of reparation.

Phallocentrism has divided the sexes, has alienated women from each other. There is a link between calling, symbolic exchange, and propriation outside of which we do not know sexuality. The manner in which one calls the other through language, in translation, is all-important for the thinking of (sexual) *differance.* As Derrida had said: "Propriation is all the more powerful since it is its process that organizes both the totality of language's process and symbolic exchange in general."[25] To escape the harshness of such an exchange, to uncover their language of innocence, women must go back to a different *appel,* a call, an appeal—not just a word but one through which resonates the English apple, *la pomme,* the fruit instrumental in the Fall, in the expulsion from the true garden of Eden, and in loss of innocence, in the law that divided the sexes. Cixous goes back through (her mother) Eve, to reread the biblical myth, a primitive scene, the first "story," now from a feminine border. Eve savors the apple; she tastes and likes it, contrary to what scriptural fathers have impressed on women. *Le beau,* the beautiful, though without a utilitarian value, is also *bon,* good and tasty. It appeals to the senses and pleasure. She does not feel the guilt. The bliss (*jouissance*) of Eve prevents her from falling into separation (death, castration, etc., etc.).

Woman, closer to her senses, tastes words before they fall under the separating authority of a symbolic order. *Daurades* without seduction, they bathe in the world as uterus, enveloping and enveloped: "When they were speaking to one another all naked without a third, they were bathing in the language which never translates: carries, does not separate, does not deport [*porte, ne sépare pas, ne déporte pas*]."[26] The verb *porter:* to carry, to transfer, rather than the noun *porte:* a dividing, separating door. If there are scenes, there are no symbolic closures to fence them in. To write is analogous to a rhythmic gliding through the waters where one is already in the other: "Listen: Accord Koré to Cordelia—by Kor, by sympathy, by correspondences: the elements of this searching story are searching stories—and if this story is that of a writing, of a woman addressing herself in flesh and in song to a she, searching for her and addressing her, and while singing coasts closely the border of the sea, then she has at least three elements. Do you follow us? Coast her, coast me)."[27] The paragraph enveloped in its matrical, parenthetical plenitude, being both in and out, mimes the rolling movement of the *ronde* which inscribes Koré in Cordelia through a bodily structure. In myth, both women were suffering; in syntax, Cordélia is a *corps-délit,* a criminal body, the crime of having a body, a bodily idea. That which unbinds, *délie,* has taken on some more matter since *Prénoms de personne. Corps d'elle il y a;* a body of she there is, or *corde il y a:* there is a thread, which links Koré to Cordelia, a thread that is never cut between mother and daughter, between *elle* and *elle,* she and she. Also, *corps-ai,* body I have, and cor = *coeur,* the heart, the seat of feeling or, in a Heideggerian sense, source and shelter: "The heart [*Gemüt*] is the source and shelter, the binding and the voice of this '*muot*' which exposes us to the intimate depth where the heart takes on the figure of patience and poverty, softness and nobility, grace and generosity, magnanimity and longanimity."[28] Accord *Koré* to *Co*rdelia, in a musical accord, through voice.

At the crossings of Heidegger and Clarice Lispector, Cixous insists on poverty—not that which Nietzsche had criticized in the concept, but one without ornament, communication as communion, almost silent. Koré and Cordelia are not developed into characters; they are figures with little visibility other than a literal one but with many textual echoes from myth, Shakespeare,

Kierkegaard, and Freud. *To accord:* to make agree, to put in harmony, to agree grammatically. *By sympathy:* from *sym,* with, and *pathy,* feeling and pathos. *By correspondence: cor* contains the sound of the heart; *cor-respond,* to call with, to answer, to write to, refers to mail and letters. Koré and Cordelia vibrate in each other without killing each other. The poetic search is a calling of the other, who is touched and caressed—or *effleuré*—with flowery echoes. This language of plenitude would be found on the verge of disappearance, there where same and other communicate by correspondence:

> already, all of them, from their sides to their buttocks, in their thighs up to their knees, feel the soft sorrow awaken, the belt of caresses buckle and unbuckle, the womb lyre, are in bliss, suffer from having been in bliss erstwhile, from still being in bliss, from no longer being in bliss again—are drawn together for they have felt this joy, all the names of this joy, in foreign tongues, they do not know them, they would not know how to speak it, but they would know how to shudder it, to coo it, to transfuse it from hand to hand, to transmit it from breast to lips, to flow it from proximity to proximity, from mouth to breast, to pour it, to increase it with the ear.[29]

Mother, daughter (or lover) are linked by blood, not by convention, by the (name of the) law. This, Cixous asserts, leads to differences in masculine and feminine relations to the law. Again, masculine and feminine are thought of as libidinal effects, yet they tend to be polarized through the equations masculine = man and feminine = woman. Whereas the masculine position consists in either transgressing or respecting the law, the feminine simply ignores it—whence the unforgivable position of the feminine in society. To name somebody always falls within the structure of the law, but the mother calls without naming:

> —This daughter, her mother does not call her? No name to call her?
> —No, calls her without name.
> —Between mother and lover, no name. Between us. A young person without proper name to retain her, to keep her without leash, without

limit, without tie. No thread to bring back one to the other: no separation. Between them, no interruption, no anguish, no calling back, no forgetfulness. From one to the other a flow of flowers, the earth, the sea, the daughter, the going fertile with returns. Calls her: you: name of us. All the names of all that which grows sing her also, accompany her. In their baskets, the delicious immensity of distances filled with presence; to go away without leaving each other, the space inside them, as depth of proximity, the flesh of their flesh, the earth made tenderness.[30]

Cixous questions the poetic process: Who walks? No personal pronoun, no subject, no *she* who walks but always more than one. The poet must write with a multiplicity of "selves." The movement of writing starts with a *"coup d'eautre,"* which opens on a presence of otherness that nothing can interrupt, whether of time, distance, or death.

The structure of the two women giving and receiving functions as metaphor for the poetic process: the call of a woman making and receiving a call from another woman. The *don,* the gift, takes place in the *appel,* the English apple, in the milieu that assembles them. The presence of the other in the body gives sense to the poetic process. In a strange reality, on another scene, the "presence" of the other body is felt even after "separation." It is man who in his fiction reduces woman to absence. "A man a thousand times more *fort que da,*" exclaims Cixous, mocking the Freudian fort/da, in the overdetermination of *fort* as both strong and absent, quite different from that in *Les Commencements.*

Women were once beings of proximity without "why?"—a question leading to naming and the law. Again, Cixous's problematic is in dialogue with that of Jacques Derrida, who, from a "masculine" border, had questioned—in his readings of Blanchot's Orphic texts—concepts of proximity and distance in relation to the calling of *elle* (she).[31] Where Derrida suspends movement in the *pas,* both a noun and an adverb, a step and its annulment, Cixous from her feminine border asserts: "Angela . . . comes and says, 'you [*tu*] are there,' and she announces, 'you [*vous*] are there,' and truly,

I am there, in I and in her, and she is there and she arrives to me."[32] The *la* with its musical overconnotation does not have the punctual simplicity of an *ici* (here) but is space in movement. The shift from you (*tu*) to you (*vous*), writes a self already *with* other on a map where letters do (sometimes) arrive at their destination. Women sing not from loss and absence but with that which has never been lost. The difference between masculine and feminine relations to presence and absence determine their respective attitudes toward mourning, melancholia, detachment. Antigone in this respect was not a woman. Male poets and writers past and present, from Rilke to Derrida in *La Carte postale,* need a nevertheless absent woman to write. Cixous writes from presence: "I write to speak near you, in silence, after her."[33] The secret is in the closeness between life and death, lips and letters. Written caresses survive in the sense of a triumph of life.

A True Garden

Cixous urges women to write in a "natural" (yet cultural) language, a language of innocence, replacing that of the innocence of dreams, of *sainteté,* from the earlier heterosexual scenes. This art of innocence is in a sense paradoxical, since art and *techné* are always ruseful. Women must write in a language prior to words that name. In Cixous's true garden (*un vrai jardin*), the heliotrope is not troping toward the sun; the flowers are not rhetorical flowers but are there to give and receive caresses, *effleurer,* rather than the masculine violence of the hymeneal *déflorer.* The question is how to "live" a garden with words that are here before memory, death:

To enjoy blissfully a walk from the path of the summit ridge to the ground of the Garden of Essays, to make the trip faithfully, in accord with life, with body, we have to exit softly, leave all phrases of recommendation, and now live, simply live, live entirely there where we live, begin the way it begins, to let things happen according to their mode, let the rose be felt in a rose way, to descend toward the garden attracted, led by the appeal of its freshness, to descend trusting the body, the way my childhood descended, before knowing the names of the streets, but the senses know their ways, before the proper noun and the common nouns, along the perfumes, walking with feet in sandals in the heavy perfumes, in the movement of the marketplace.[34]

Cixous searches for a language of *essais*, essays of thinking and weighing; of *esse,* the Latin to be and the German to eat; *et c'est,* a language that links by a thread, far from the *et* in the celibatary machine of the post-pattern; *et sait,* and knows, a bodily knowledge with resonances of *elle sait* and *(H)él. C.,* the author's name. Knowledge is never an abstract *savoir* but a matter of flesh and blood, of all the senses: hearing, tasting, touching, and the rest.

On this map without borders, immense spaces open, and like her avatars—Gradiva, Penthesilea, Cleopatra, Cixous—Illa traverses them in winged sandals. However, the movement is in a sense reversed. The heady, airy, ascending movement of the earlier search has given way to a descending rhythm of slow meditation. The bosom (*sein*), still a privileged locus, emphasizes less the chiasmatic crossing of nipples with other nipples than the possibilities of open containment. The new writing privileges life: "There are two writings; one writes books, the other writes living."[35] To live the rose, a noun echoing from the past tense of the English verb to rise, becomes a kind of *fiat,* a coming into being of the rose. "The rose roses" is reminiscent of Heidegger's "the world worlds." The writer in bliss lets things speak in their language before translation. A phonic conflation of *fruit, frisson,* and *jouissance* (fruit, shudder, and bliss), makes the wor(l)d be. An *Obst-lese,* with resonances of obstetrics, brings selves, others, into the world.

In this writing of innocence, night and day do not conflict. The luminous night engenders day. Stars come down to earth as starry texts: "I had just put the star on earth. This child I had not written by myself, I have written it from *elles* (them), and it glowed from itself, from us. The radiance of the apples of writing is now the source of light of this paper."[36] The stars are not the unattainable, the Kantian moral imperative inscribed in everyone's heart. Stars touch the earth, there where sky and earth come together. Masculine and feminine relations to the law differ. The feminine ignores the law, whereas the masculine either accepts it or tries to ruse with it. These different effects can be read in writing practices. In a recent seminar, Cixous showed this through readings of three primal scenes that "shaped" artists: James Joyce, Maurice Blanchot, Clarice Lispector. The qualifiers, masculine and feminine, are now divided between men and women. Joyce is the great transgressor. He is "mixed up" with the law all the time. She finds the "beginning" of Joyce's work and his relation to the law in a sentence from *Portrait of the Artist:* "O, Stephen will apologize." The message of the law is given by the mother, who, rather than prescribing an interdiction, speaks as if the son had already transgressed and asks him to apologize. Hence a relation of guilt and a need to transgress. In Blanchot's *Ecriture du désastre,* in another primitive scene, the boy "unstars the sky" (*dés-astre*), which he realizes is only an idea, not a reality. The boy discovers that the starry sky of the moral law in "reality" is black; he knows that there is nothing, but as a boy he still functions within the limits of the law. In Lispector, by contrast, there is no law other than that imposed on us by the institutions. In *Near the Wild Heart,* the little girl, reprimanded by her aunt for shoplifting, replies (in essence): "What I have done would be evil if I had done it with a feeling of evil and fear. But I have no fear. I take it upon myself. I have willfully and consciously taken the book." It is out of such a position of ignorance of guilt that a *féminin futur* must write itself.

A "Book of Hours": With ou l'art de l'innocence

To write and live in innocence close to one's origins requires a different temporal mode, a succession not of hours, cutting, dividing, but of the breathing (*respiration*) of a living "being" (with "being") travailed by questions. "Hour," rather than referring to passing of time, must be read in a medieval sense of prayer as in a "book of hours." Cixous writes a quest, in a strong sense, of how to live without being limited by the law, fear, unhappiness in a poetic, not an abstract, way. Similar preoccupations underlie all of her texts, though questions are asked differently in her more recent work. The violent explosions of excess, exuberance, beauty in the early texts have given way to a more meditative approach with a new chain— joy, happiness, patience, grace, poverty—as Bataille (Hegel and Nietzsche) is replaced by Heidegger. Cixous continues to question our relation to knowledge through her writing of innocence. Fiction, once a projection of the *non-encore-là,* has given way to texts that explore the "desirable," or all that is not known and that we do not want to know. It is "situated" in incomprehension of that of which we are innocent. This requires a way of speaking and writing on the other side of learned knowledge, open but not ignorant. Not a silence, *after* the word, but a "word" before the word. The text radiates its own colored lights: "At the beginning the vibrations are intensely blueyellow in a wake of peppery perfume, with an edge, heliotropic, and the last syllables are confused with the breeze."[37] Colors go beyond their spatial limits and the articulate drives of the unconscious. Colors are sexualized and should, at the limit, replace qualifiers like masculine and feminine.

A language of this double innocence requires a textual composition where the author is always more than one, where there is not one *signataire,* one victor, but where there is a dialogue of multiple voices. This Cixous carries out in *With ou l'art de l'innocence.* It is woven around a suspended name H (Hélène?), *hache*—both as ax and mute letter—who, in the position of author, is tormented by guilt and dreams of liberation but is limited by *interdits* from the outside or by those she has interiorized; Cordelia, carried over from *Illa,* the ill-fated heroine from the Shakespearean stage whose love for a man is exploited (Cixous asserts that one could generalize and speak of a cordelian structure, since many women in society occupy that position); *Aura* (or Hora), the one who bathes in the aura of a *féminin futur.* There are masculine "characters" as well, occupying different libidinal positions. The text becomes a dialogue, in a

Heideggerian sense, in which various selves help one another overcome inner resistances that slow down transfer or make it impossible. The text does not lead to a result. The other is never "vanquished" or repressed. Contradictions remain as contradictions. If one character stops, another can go further. Through communication with others, the impossible is freed; interior limits traverse the inside of the texts, not simply as margins. From one character to the next, communication is established through vibration. Since speaking is always done from the center, other characters who can see from the sides are drawn in to displace limits.

With ou l'art de l'innocence questions the possibility of happiness in a society of surveillance and suffering. It asserts the drive to life—stronger than death—which Cixous, following Heidegger, calls a miracle or grace. The drive to life does not allow despair about one's own or someone else's suffering. It is an affirmation of a pure athletic life, almost superhuman in terms of acceptation. In Cixous's early texts, we read superhumanness as an attribute of the bionic woman jumping off her *Effel* tower. The same attribute refers now to the affirmation of life of the writer, who is nevertheless afflicted by suffering.

The text's development is not a structured narration with beginning, middle, and end, a willful ordering of the universe. Life is not a linear story; it is made up of moments arriving, presenting themselves, and of waiting periods. There are no violent cuts. The text, therefore, is not divided into chapters; rather it is carried by certain movements and moments where one glides from one textual region to the next. On this text-map one can travel and arrive at a destination. While there are many possible ways of arriving, the political question remains: who arrives where?

For Cixous, there are masculine and feminine modes of arriving. They are determined by the mode of arrival of the child. To men, children happen from the outside; hence their astonishment. To women, they arrive from the inside, after a period of gestation, of waiting. The relationship to the other is modified by this experience and by the effects of *jouissance* inscribed on the body. "Feminine" and "masculine" seemingly once more refer to woman and man in their sexually marked bodies, but as we will read, all the terms are used metaphorically, inserted in a new chain. Contrary to many feminists who extol the position of daughter and insist on killing the mother, Cixous ascertains that such a position nourishes the masculine phantasm of a father-daughter rapport, with its inevitable implications of rape. It is a masculine structure which—from Freud to contemporary analysts—devalorizes the mother, vitiates the mother-daughter relation in a political economy privileging the phallus.

The relation between inside and outside differs for men and women. Displacing the old symbol of woman-as-house and the masculine phantasm of being-in-woman = being-inside, Cixous ascertains that women have a different relation to the inside, since theirs is livable. Men, on the contrary, have to live in the other; the other does not live in them. Since Cixous's enterprise is textual, she reads the effects of these differences in artistic texts. As we have seen, anatomy does not *command* certain structures, and we are always already in language. Nevertheless, she cannot avoid a certain polarization with consequences in the "real." This may be due to the constraints of writing in association with the political pressures around Des Femmes.

In Cixous's text, the question of the *inside* is written in a passage of initiation, half hallucinatory, revelatory, almost ritualistic, intimate. It is an "intimate passage" into the bosom of a woman. The bosom, not the phallic object of desire but a nourishing, flowing *sein,* may be replaced by voice. We are touched by voice because we are enveloped by it and can enter into it. Haunted by *dedans,* in relation to the possibilities of imprisonment and *sortie,* Cixous can finally realize through voice and musicalization of letters the paradox of her childhood, to exit and to be dedans. This is what she calls "homosexuality" among women.

Domina, the matronly mistress, replaces the hysterical Dora of previous years. Domina's knowledge flows from her breast, from her mystery. The name of mystery approaches the mystery of femininity. "The mystery of being a woman is: one and only, woman, is not alone; mystery is always of the body in the body of a woman."[38] The languages of innocence-in-liberty are those of southern countries and of summers that blend with the vivid colors and heavy perfumes of Cixous's North African scene: "Feel the tingling heat of the immense, take your fill with air in three lights, hold back your breath, and with the might of all your flesh in the dry red and reds of noon, listen! 'Woman' is the exterior name of the full."[39] Woman may refer to man. It refers to all that is full, pregnant with life, engendering. "Woman," like night engendering day, gives birth to "man." The sexualizing article *la* (the) is not part of the language of innocence. "You did not know anything but you felt it all; the earth was one, and earth is woman. And lying on the warmth of the earth, you impregnated with its vegetal incense, you, ignorant but taught by impregnation, you in the mystery of her mystery, you were breathing and you were comprised."[40]

The real *sortie* is a descent into the *sein,* the bosom of being whose mysterious qualities supersede those of the earlier oneiric spaces. Voice, heart, or soul may substitute for bosom. It refers to the space of mystery, a full space engendering life. The relation to knowledge is one *par corps,* by body and heart, not *par coeur,* from memory: "I know her by heart (or body) and that which happens to me is as if I knew two beings which are the same person but impose themselves separately and differently: because there *is* [*es gibt*]. She herself, that is to say the mystery behind her face, this profound, fresh, singing space, inexhaustible source of sources, and in which I advance, meditating, as in a starred cathedral of night. But her body I know as if I had made it with my hands, by divination, erring. I live it, the way it is, so full and strong all breathing."[41]

To Write in Silence and Plenitude: Limonade tout était si infini

One of Cixous's texts "entitled" with an enigmatic sentence from Kafka's notebooks, "*Limonade tout était si infini* [*Limonade es war alles so grenzenlos*]*,*" pushes to an extreme this economy of love through gift. Alluding to a "scene" of the pure gift told by Max Brod in which Kafka bows in front of a blind poet, Oskar Baum, in such a way that his hair touches the poet, who knows that Kafka has bowed, Cixous ascertains that there was no look, no word; all was silence.

The insistence is on the silent gift that does not come back to the sender and on a life lived to its fullest, a pure life without interruptions, without deaths, such as that of a political condemned to death in Dostoevski. In the days remaining before his execution, he leads a life without waste, without moments of interruption. Such a life of precision, where each word, each syllable is as important as every instant, where the sense of an ending is a beginning, is a true *survie*.

The scene is not one of solitude but one where a silent self and another communicate with words as light and transparent as dragonflies, fluttering, shuddering, there where the first letter is also the last sentence and where the answer, the *parce que*, is the question. The scene in a nuptial chamber is without limits, without symbolic walls, in a silent accord:

Delicacy [*délicatesse*] in two: to be in accord never to speak of a secret thing [*chose secrète*] which we share [*partageons*], because it is so fragile. But to be in accord without a word; the accord too is silent.

Because the sublime understanding [*entente*] is to accord to each other full silence: the gift of the without-word.

Delicacy of the silence pregnant with what one could say. Because happiness is not to say it: it is to be able to say.[42]

Happiness is not the syntax of a *sans*, a without, but of the without-word. It is to prehear, to taste delicately (délica*tesse*, from the German *essen*, to eat, the Latin to be) the *de* of this *de*cision to "begin" a reading through taste, as in the story of Eve. This "crime" of innocence (*délit*) that unbinds and takes out of the bed in a silent accord, in a matrix full of, or pregnant with, all that can be, all the possibles before the cutting decision of a choice. The accord links with an invisible thread, joins the hearts. The whole paragraph works on "to be," but there is no phenomenon, no coming into light, no shadow. The *partage,* the separation, is a sharing: *partageons; parce* que, the causality, is more like a continuity where one is already in the other, where the answer is the question.

Silence spaces and links. Silence is pregnant with all the possibles, with the limitless, with all that could be without the cruelty of choice, decisions, that *de* of each *coup de dé* that never will abolish chance, yet will decide for one of the sides in a dice roll.

In one of her most recent texts, "August 12, 1980," Cixous writes from another birth scene. Her communion with Clarice Lispector, who is also from a southern country, makes Cixous experience the heat of the Brazilian landscape, intense like fire. "It must be so hot that the mystery explodes like a pine cone."[43] For those born in such heat, the supreme value is water, not gold. The inside of water is the truth. Truth quenches thirst; it is not in the circulation of money and its association with the phallus but in the flowing currents of (birth) water. The lack of water is felt as a kind of feminine castration. "Because all she does is from source, each thing coming from her revives a thirsty emotion. Even when she takes a tropical bus, everybody croaks with apathy and therefore lets everyone die, and here it happens that without rock, without stick, without gods, in the same will, she makes a fountain spring forth. This does not make her a saint, and clearly some people are not in want of her water."[44] The desire for a springing forth of water, or heretofore of milk, for a life-giving source, recurs in what function like primal scenes in Cixous's texts.

Yet her need for a language before translation and metaphor, before taking the bus ("the tropical bus too cruelly real"), might be dictated in part by a certain desire to write out of guilt, to *exit* from the imperative of the law that made her take a taxi one day, as a child, when a man asked her for drinking money. As a child, Cixous refused to give the money to quench the man's thirst; with her golden pieces she paid for a taxi to take her home because she did not want to dirty her white sandals. The scene functions as a scene of guilt, an encounter with the law. Haunted by the latter, Cixous writes texts of traversal, on winged sandals, in search of a double innocence. The scene may also be read as Cixous's questioning of her own writing activities, her desire to write *with* presence, as a writing-out of a certain guilt for not quenching the thirst but taking the metaphoric vehicle instead. Writing even *with* presence is nevertheless based on a certain absence, and the writer continues to be haunted by the unresolved questions: Who pays when I write? Whom do I kill? How can I get away from narcissistic gratification and from the structure of the law?

5

Toward a Promethean "Féminin Futur"

From Cixous's euphoric belief in social revolution through linguistic revolution to her more meditative "magic" writings, the textual endeavors are constant: to displace a constraining, limiting, hyper-coded language into languages-in-liberty; to rethink writing activities in terms of absence, presence; to reduce the former; to displace sexual opposition into a play of differences; to change desire of recognition based on death into one of affirmation and love.

Some of the difficulties in reading Cixous may come from the relationship between theory and praxis in her texts. *Literature,* a term once decried during the *Tel Quel* era, is nevertheless an ultimate, tonic term in her writing. The insistence is on the poetic—on a political poetic—where the word does not point to a signified but takes itself for object. But this writing does have a political goal-in-movement. As such, it has a message and a referent: to revalorize "women" who had been repressed and forgotten. In some of Cixous's writings, this leads almost to a new allegory, that of the goodness of woman, of women.

What sets Cixous apart from other women writers—poets or theoreticians—is the intricate part played by theory *and* poetry. Her writings are infused with and written from contemporary theory—mainly written by men—which she turns toward women. Many of her writings seem to be "feminine" answers to Derrida's more "masculine" readings. Where Derrida insisted on decapitating paternal authority, Cixous from her border unburies a repressed maternal. The emphasis is on the qualifiers rather than on the nouns "father," "mother," with echoes of an oedipal scenario. Maternal, generous, overflowing: these are qualifiers of an affective economy of love. Differences between paternal and maternal are to be thought of on the level of *jouissance,* of pleasure. They do not refer to an anatomical organ, since the body is always a ciphered body. However, they are inscribed in a comparison. Cixous ascertains the superiority of a "feminine" poetic writing over a "masculine" theoretical discourse. She decries the latter as systematic, closed, limited by laws; she praises her own medium: artistic writing. Her medium allows her to be freer, to do away with the constraints and shackles of theoretical discourse, even one that works on excess. This allows her to slip in and out of theory, to bypass some of its "rigor" in favor of greater textual freedom. Yet as pedagogue and academic at Paris VIII, Cixous carries on a theoretical discourse in her as yet unpublished lectures. What sets her apart from other "feminist" theoreticians—all of whom revalorize woman—is precisely that poetic *plus value* of pleasure she offers the reader as a gift in her writings.

From the summit-readings that unbind (*dé-lie*) to the readings, writings of a *corps-délie,* that non-name of bodily "presence," to those of Tasso's *Jerusalem Delivered,* a Jerusalem *dé-livrée,* freed, delivered, unclothed, no longer a book, a gender, the preoccupations are similar. Yet the *de*cisions of each reading and writing are in constant movement and transformation. From Gradiva to Penthesilea, from Cleopatra to Demeter and Clorinda, Cixous's endeavor is to read and (re)write the feminine in its play with other feminines, other masculines. From the position of daughter in a masculine structure to that of mother-daughter celebrating women (*des femmes*), the quest now moves toward a writing beyond genre, sexual or literary. A (feminine, maternal) affective economy of gift and love is no longer reserved to women alone. In "Tancrède continue," a reading of Tasso, the positions of man and woman are infinitely destabilized, interchangeable. Clorinda, draped as warrior, and Tancredi are caught in history, in politics. They must oppose each other, combat each other, but underneath halter and cuirass the frankness of the lovers is stronger than death. "Two camps quarrel about the body of the Beloved [*La Bien-Aimée*]. I mean Jerusalem. Two camps. Always the same. Today as in the times of the crusades and as in Paradise."[1]

What interests Cixous is the story under history, the story of the other and the other of the other, not that of the couple and the same: "Not Renaud and Armide, couple-of-the-same. But the Others, the overflowing, Tancredi, Clorinda, the lovers of frankness, these two singular creatures, stronger than they, yes, capable one [*l'une*] and the other of going, at the price of life, for the love of truth, of love, beyond their own strength, to the other—the most distant and the closest. The two always other, who dare to accomplish this departure, exit [*Sortie*]."[2] The couple, contained, limited, gives way in Clorinda and Tancredi to a same always other, always moving toward another, animated by a violent movement of love, a swing of the pendulum similar to that of Kleist's puppets. There, *il* and *elle,* he and she, are destabilized, are drifting from one to the other border.

"I read *Jerusalem Delivered,* with lost bodies, with disquieted bodies, unlimited bodies." A reading of the sublime without measure, yet of the sensible.[3] Faithful to herself, Cixous speaks of undoing laws, limits. This is not to say that there is *no* law, *no* limit. But reversing the philosophical emphasis of displacing limits in a movement of retreat, of *é-loignement,* Cixous insists on advancing toward the other, toward the infinitely small, with the freedom that a poetic writing gives her.

How does one love (the other)? How does one give? How does one receive? The question of the gift in relation to affective economies has been a constant throughout Cixous's writings; they all meditate on ways of loving. How does one love without killing the other? Love is linked to time and space. It is a question of listening to the other, of being attuned to the other. Contrary to passion, which burns all the steps and kills, the movement of love toward the other is full of moments of non-love. Cixous maintains her distinction from *Prénoms de personne,* between *consumer* (to burn) and *consommer* (to eat, to incorporate). In love, there may be moments of non-love as well as of passion, moments of consuming. But there cannot be *consommation,* which in any case is death.

The most difficult part is to keep the love in movement, to remove it from a dialectic of *avoir, non-avoir,* linked to possession. Such a free, burning, Promethean love for the other, a love that respects the other's enigma, that does not want to *know* the other, is written in this passage of love and desire between two "women" in constant metamorphoses. Noting the minute vibrations of a love song shuddered, cooed, reminiscent of the magic tales of *A Thousand and One Nights,* Cixous writes the comings and goings, ebbings and flowings of a desire—slow and patient or violent, aggressive, and bloody—of a love, a life lived to its fullest. There, the other is not just a word, an absent other, and the word does not come back to the same in narcissistic gratification; rather, the word is attached to a a body, touches another body, in an endless movement of giving and receiving. More than a passage *of* the infinite between gift and debt, it is an arriving *at* the infinite:

There is why I said: Come! with such a superhuman impetuosity. I have said "come," naked [*nu*] and clear, and nothing more, as if I were a tyrant. I threw my order out of the window, but in truth, yes, I have put my heart in it, it is my heart I put in it for Promethea, my own heart thrown out of the upstairs window like an order, like a gift; it falls like a stone toward the earth, falls straight toward the center of the earth, and at the bottom is Promethea . . . and if Promethea did not hold out her hands, the apple would be smashed, the blood of the child would spill.[4]

H in accord with Promethea sings an affirmative song of love, not of double affirmation and mourning, not directed against the authority of a father, but a free song, *un et nu,* of the limitless: "Promethea is a woman? Yes. Is a mare? Yes. Is also a Yes. Yes to everything I want. To everything? Yes. To everything I want to pursue, try, feel. Yes. That is why passing through her I arrive at the infinite.[5]

Appendix: An Exchange with Hélène Cixous[1]

H. C. The preliminary question is that of a "feminine writing," itself a dangerous and stylish expression full of traps, which leads to all kinds of confusions. True, it is simple to say "feminine writing." The use of the word "feminine"—I believe I have discussed it at length elsewhere—is one of the curses of our times. First of all, words like "masculine" and "feminine" that circulate everywhere and that are completely distorted by everyday usage,—words which refer, of course, to a classical vision of sexual opposition between men and women—are our burden, that is what burdens us. As I often said, my work in fact aims at getting rid of words like "feminine" and "masculine," "femininity" and "masculinity," even "man" and "woman," which designate that which cannot be classified inside of a signifier except by force and violence and which goes beyond it in any case. So it is true that when one says "feminine writing," one could almost think in terms of graphology. One could say, it is the writing of an elegant woman, she is this or that. That is obviously not what is at stake. Instead of saying feminine writing or masculine writing, I ended up by saying a writing said to be feminine or masculine, in order to mark the distance. In my seminar, rather than taking this elementary precaution, I speak of a decipherable libidinal femininity which can be read in a writing produced by a male or a female. The qualifier masculine or feminine which I use for better or for worse comes from the Freudian territory.

v. c. What do you mean by "libidinal"?

H. C. Something extremely precise which has been defined by Freud in his numerous writings on libido. It is something which can be defined from the body, as the movement of a pulsion toward an object, and which is part of the discoveries that may be defined as the Freudian discoveries *par excellence*. It allows us to know what in other times had been analyzed as the treaty of passions. This is what I refer to, and I believe that the word "economy" is important. It is the regime of that which in the past used to be called the effect of desire, of love. It is the love life in fact, or the sexual life, which is regulated by energy marked psychically by the subject, which is lived consciously, and which can be described as economic metaphors with moments of investment in passion, love, disgust, or anything else, moments of disinvestments from subject to object. These are libidinal investments, which can be treated and spoken about in morals or philosophy as well. For example, the possibility of giving, of generosity, or as one says in common terms, of the seven deadly sins, of avarice, which is not to give, to retain. All these are effects or denominations of things that are entirely to be thought of in the category of libidinal economies.

Then, we need qualifiers to clarify the types of regimes, and the ones we use are, once again, in spite of everything, "feminine" and "masculine." Why? True, it is a question here of our whole history, of our whole culture; true, it would be nice if one could use, instead of masculine and feminine, color adjectives, for example. Like blue and green and black; I said that in a text. True, one could also displace across political economy and say, for example, capitalist or I do not know what else. One could take notions that have been disengaged by the socioethnologists who talk about potlatch, like Mauss. You see, these are linguistic instruments, words that do not take into account the reality of exchange. Still, why does one say masculine and feminine? And what does it signify? Because the first exchanges, the primary exchanges—I do not say originary, because obviously there is no origin—are distinguished in our first milieu, the familial milieu, for example. They take place among people of different sexes, but what we also know with Freud, since Freud, though it was known before him and can be read in literary texts, is that human beings who can be distinguished anatomically in an obvious way—which leads to I.D. cards and social roles—are not, at the level of sexual economies, as different as that. All human beings are originally bisexual; that is why in my theoretical childhood I have been led to use this word. We know that the child is not as categorically determined as that. When children grow up, they learn to identify with the adult model of man or woman. Yet these identificatory determinations are belated, and there is a whole period which Freud describes when there is a bisexual potential. This does not mean homosexual with the tendency one may think. Just as there is always, in every human being, a complex relationship between death drives and life drives, there is a complex relationship between different libidinal economies which would be passive and active, constantly binding and unbinding themselves, exchanging, spending, and retaining.

I can use the analytic vocabulary, since I do not have to enclose myself in its system: oral, anal, genital. A full, total, accomplished individual goes through all the stages and arrives at the genital stage that assembles everything. As for the intermediary stages, one knows, for example with Freud, that the anal stage corresponds to an anal economy, which is an avaricious economy of retention, of hard exchange. There are people in whom there is a dominance, an insistence. They stop at a certain stage, at the oral stage, for example, and have a censoring relationship to others. The ideal harmony, reached by few, would be genital, assembling everything and being capable of generosity, of spending. That is what I mean when I speak of *écriture féminine,* that is what I talk about. Of course, it is not exactly me; it is the inscription of something that carries in everyday language the determination of the provisional name of femininity, and which refers precisely to something that I would like to define in the way of an economy, of production, of bodily effects of which one can see a great number of traits.

For example, last year in my seminar we worked on texts by Lispector. We worked on the fact that her texts are very humid texts, that in them it is always a question of something humid. I would even say that one of her major texts, *Agua Viva*, is like water. Can one write water, can one read water? How can one do it? That is precisely the question of this text. One can do it only by throwing oneself into the water, by becoming one with the water. To show the difference, I also had recourse to masculine texts that present traits of masculine economy and that insist in the most remarkable way on drying up. I say purposely "drying up," which is done by something wet that dries. I do not say something absolutely dry. I am not going to oppose the desert and the sea, not at all. But I want to work on the level of an economic differential, on that, for example, which is of the domain of the humid. We also know that the humid is vital, that absolute dryness prevents one from living. I had taken a text, and that is where we will have to take a number of precautions. I had chosen the most extraordinary text and the easiest to read, Blanchot's text in general and this one in particular. It is a text which he had produced in *L'Ecriture du désastre,* the writing of *dis-aster,* a text that goes toward a drying up. The writer will never cry again. He has shed all the tears. There is secretion, etc., and then there is an episode, there is an event, a symbolic and decisive event, which decides the masculine orientation, which determines that this child, who at first is neutral (we do not know whether it is masculine or feminine) orients itself toward the decision of belonging to the masculine gender. One can analyze this decision in other texts by Blanchot. I have done it at length elsewhere.

When I read this text to you, I did not want to tell you at first who wrote it. Because if I do tell you, for example, that it is by Maurice Blanchot, I am saying that it is a text written by a man and you are sent back to the lure, to the screen. You are sent back to the fact that it is a man who wrote a masculine text. My own position is to insist always on the fact that libidinal femininity is not the *propre* of women and that libidinal masculinity is not the *propre* of men.

What is most important for me, what allows me to continue to live and not to despair, is precisely the conviction that it does not depend on the anatomical sex, not on the role of man and of woman, but that it depends in fact on life's chance, which is everybody's responsibility. For example, this year in my seminar we work on a double corpus, on Clarice Lispector and on Kleist. In reality, the texts are interchangeable because Kleist is absolutely exceptional. Kleist produces a work that functions in a more feminine than masculine way. That means he is capable of spending at all levels, of displacing the rhythms, for example, of the living, of the relationship between life and death, of all that which could be qualified more easily as feminine than masculine. So I say, taking all my precautions, that in fact the ideal for me would be to use "proper" names instead of adjectives, feminine and masculine: to speak of a Kleistian economy would be much better. When I am obligated to theorize, when one asks me to theorize in order to clarify my ideas, I find myself back in the trap of words.

Of course, there is a certain danger for us in taking up words which are so strongly marked. That is why, in my seminar, I do not use them. But publicly, I must constantly have recourse to them, because we are in history, we live in history, we are in a historical, political situation which we must take into account. Literature does not float like a planet in air. It is part of "truth" even if I consider that its part is precisely to precede, to anticipate ordinary reality, to distance itself from it, to go faster than it. We must take into account the fact that we are caught in daily reality in the stories of men and women, in the stories of a role. That is why I come back to the question of the terms masculine and feminine. Why these words? Why do they stay with us? Why do we not reject them? Because in spite of everything and for historical reasons, the economy said to be feminine—which would be characterized by features, by traits, that are more adventurous, more on the side of spending, riskier, on the side of the body—is more livable in women than in men. Why? Because it is an economy which is socially dangerous in our times. That is what we saw already with Kleist. You live, you believe, you give life to values that are apparently moral values, but in fact these moral values do not exist without precisely coming forth from a primary locus which is in any case corporeal. If, for example, like Kleist, you believe in the possibility of a love, a real love, not one based on a power struggle, on a daily war, on the enslavement of one by the other, society is going to reject you. If you are a man, the rejection is almost immediate. Society does not give you any time. You have just lived through an experience, and society tells you that if you believe that, you should get lost; there is no place for you. What you are doing is absolutely prohibited, and you are sent into madness and death. Women do have another chance. They can indulge in this type of life because by definition and for culturally negative reasons they are not called upon, they are not obligated, to participate in the big social *fête*—which is phallocentric—since they are often given places in the shadow, places of retreat, where they are in fact parked. It will be more easily accepted that a woman does not battle, does not want power. A man will not be forgiven.

v. c. Yes, but do women not want to get out of that negative historical position?

H. c. Something which is absolutely necessary. What I am saying is always on two levels. One level would be, if you like, that of libidinal truth. It is cut mercilessly by historical reality. I also say that for negative reasons, women have positive reasons to save something through generosity which is mortal for men. Because man is projected on a scene where he has to be a warrior among warriors. He is assigned to the scene of castration. He must defend his phallus; if not, it is death. There you are. Women are not called upon the scene of castration, which in a way is not good for them, since they are repressed. Let us suppose that in our feminist period, women manage, for example, to have equal chances; that is precisely where things start to become interesting and complicated. With equal chances, you are back in the old scenes. In the old scenes there were power struggles, and so what does one do? That is our problem. That is the problem of all women who, for example, cross the bar of absolute repression behind which women are parked and who are, in fact, on the side of men. What do they do? Either they are killed right away, or they effectively resist castration. They find themselves in the scenes where castration makes the law with the usual phallic stakes. But what about us? What we like, what we want, what men may also want but have been taught a long time ago to renounce— are we going to keep that? That is when one begins to live dramas. Are we going to be the equals of men, are we going to be as phallic as they are? Or do we want to save something else, something more positive, more archaic, much more on the side of *jouissance,* of pleasure, less socializable? If so, how and at what price? That is our daily question.

You see, somebody like Kleist was on the one hand called upon to be a man, since he was in the military. He was in the normal, phallic space reserved for men. At the same time, he cannot renounce something entirely different, which he himself calls paradise. And he wonders: does this paradise have a chance in our world, which is purgatory or hell? He attempted to give this idea of paradise a chance, and he lost. But obviously, this idea of paradise is a very good metaphor, since the paradise of Eve is that which is defined by an immediate relation women have to *jouissance* and another type of knowledge. Kleist believes in it, but if there is prohibition, it is because there is law and the masculine world, which permanently deals with repressing this paradise that is always there and always ready to come back again.

v. c. One of women's demands is nevertheless to enter society.

h. c. That is our problem. We can no longer bear the situation of repression, of desocialization, of desymbolization, of inferiority, but we lose both ways. Is it possible to win? Yes, of course. But what a struggle. It is true that if we enter society to become men, we have lost everything. In this case, we leave the space of repression to win another repression, which will please men who are also wasting their lives. Can one win? Only on condition that upon entering society one does not identify with men but that one works on other possibilities of living, on other modes of life, on other relationships to the other, other relationships to power, etc., in such a way that one also brings about transformations in oneself, in others, and in men. That is a long project.

v. c. And very difficult, the more so as women do not have the means of power to make transformations in a society which is more open to those who are in power.

h. c. True. In any event, we can work only on compromise, a word that is always enunciated in the negative mode, but that has to be displaced. I do not believe in sexual opposition nor in a sexuality that would be strictly feminine or strictly masculine, since there are always traces of originary bisexuality. And then, there is exchange. As soon as you simply touch the other, you alter the other and you are altered by the other, an alteration that may be positive or negative. It is negative if there is compromise, if you are incorporated by the other, etc. Yet there are modalities of exchange that are respectful modalities, where you let yourself be sufficiently altered to feel the other of the other—not too much, because then you destroy yourself.

v. c. Are you saying that one must be between the two? Is that why you come back to the position of compromise?

h. c. No, I am not between. Be very careful. That is precisely where I would be most careful. The between, the *entre,* is the neither-one-nor-the-other. I am not of the neither-one-nor-the-other. I am rather on the side of *with,* in spite of all the difficulties and confusions this may bring about. It is hard to keep an equilibrium which, to use the word I use all the time, must be graceful. It has to be moving, has to be in movement. As soon as you stop, that is it. One must constantly work to keep this equilibrium in movement. I do not know whether what I say is clear enough.

v. c. What then would be the strategic "goal" of a feminine writing?

h. c. That is where I would come back to the fact that the word "feminine"—which I put between 150 quotation marks to prevent it from being used in the mode of a "feminine woman," as in fashion magazines—qualifies nevertheless a certain type of economy, the traits of which I analyze for myself as positive traits. I consider that every person should have an interest, individually and politically, not in fighting them but on the contrary in developing them. When I work on this question, I always do so from a literary corpus, because it is easier, let us say. You spoke to me, for example, of separation and reparation. I think that, if you like, a feminine libidinal economy is an economy which has a more supple relation to property, which can stand separation and detachment, which signifies that it can also stand freedom—for instance, the other's freedom. So to take a ridiculous example, the conjugal situation is that of appropriation; it is an initiation of appropriation: I am no longer myself, I belong to you, etc. As soon as there is appropriation in a rigid mode, you may be sure that there is going to be incorporation. It destroys the possibility of being other. It is the arrest of freedom of the other, and that is enormous. A feminine libidinal economy, one that tolerates the movements of the other, is very rare: one that tolerates the comings and goings, the movements, the *écart* [space, interval, gap]. So how is this going to work in a literary text? You will have literary texts that tolerate all kinds of freedom—unlike the more classical texts—which are not texts that delimit themselves, are not texts of territory with neat borders, with chapters, with beginnings, endings, etc., and which will be a little disquieting because you do not feel the arrest, the edge [the *arrêt* or the *arête*].

v. c. What is the scope of this feminine writing?

H. C. To touch upon feminine writing frees, liberates language, word usage. Of course, one cannot imagine a political liberation without a linguistic liberation; that is all very banal. It is evident, everyone knows it. It is not by chance that all the regional movements grab on to their language. It is in order to escape, if you would like, the language of the father. It is in order to take something from a language which would be less authoritarian. It is a lot of work.

V. C. When you talk about the other, you draw in an ethical dimension. What is the relationship you see between an ethical and a political dimension, between a political dimension and respect for the other?

H. C. It is the same thing, though it depends on what one means by political. In the sense of management, it becomes a technical question which in any event refers back to a political question. Otherwise, for me, there is only ethics, nothing else.

V. C. What about political in the sense of a community, of a *polis*, or city with its own police force? When you talk about "women," even between quotation marks, you still refer to a very specific group with its demands and ideas of community. There are new exclusions, new masters.

H. C. The problem goes beyond that of women. It is the problem of any community, any society, because there have been many ideal societies. One collides right away with a contradiction that is not mastery. I will take it at a banal level. When we founded Paris VIII, at the time of '68, we founded it with the idea that there would be no more professors, no more masters—something that never did materialize, because if one is not the master, the other is, of course. We never did get out of the Hegelian system. What one can do is displace it as much as possible. One has to fight it; one can diminish the degree of mastery, yet without completely eliminating it. There always must be a tiny bit of phallus, so that things continue one way or the other. I believe that it is humanly impossible to have an absolute economy without a minimum of mastery. The problem is that one is always with the regime of the maximum and not that of the minimum. But we know that organized society has done violence to everybody, that it enslaves everybody. This is not to be eliminated with complete freedom which, in my opinion, ends up by being too vague and is found only in spiritual evasion.

V. C. In the same context, you use an admirable chiasm: "poetically political, politically poetic."

H. C. I defend myself by saying that.

V. C. I read a couple of days ago, in a book by a Marxist critic, that "political" and "poetic" are irreconcilable.

H. C. People who are into politics cannot *not* say such things. People who are poets, to use a general term, but who at the same time have a political concern are obligated to say the opposite. For the latter, the poetic must have a political value: of course, it must not be an easy solution. It is not sufficient to write to be poetic. It is true, though, that you have works that think themselves and write themselves poetically without forgetting the political question. For example, Clarice Lispector constantly raises the question of politics while saying, I am not a militant politician. But it is a question that is always there, from which I determine myself. There are others: Kleist does nothing but that. All his texts are completely historical. He constantly asks questions that are political, that are treated politically. I try to do the same. I would lie if I said that I am a political woman, not at all. In fact, I have to assemble the two words, political and poetic. Not to lie to you, I must confess that I put the accent on poetic. I do it so that the political does not repress, because the political is something cruel and hard and so rigorously real that sometimes I feel like consoling myself by crying and shedding poetic tears. That is why I wrote the text called *With ou l'art de l'inno-cence*. I think that I am constantly guilty, for example, of having the privilege of being able to console myself poetically. Besides, I never console myself; as soon as I console myself, I punish myself. I think that is the paradox and the torment of people who have a calling to write that is stronger than anything else, and who know and do not forget—because most people do forget—that as soon as one writes, one betrays someone or something.

That is what Kafka thought, when he asked himself whether he had the right to write or to marry. He made those two columns with additions, subtractions, constantly realizing that he could not choose but that he had to choose and that he could not *not* choose. And finally, the choice was made. He did not do it himself, and it was always made in the direction of writing. It was not a happy choice. Finally, writing chose him until he died. He paid, of course, with death. It is true that when somebody writes, somebody dies. It may be you. When you write, it may be only you. Kafka killed others, and then at a later moment he was the one who died. He could no longer contribute to killing his fiancée. Of course, there is an easy solution which at the same time is the most difficult in the world: that is, that you die rather than the other. You see, this means that there is only death. Obviously, that is what I cannot admit. True, it is a mixture of death and life, but I think that one should die for something, in order for something to live or for something that will give life to somebody else.

v. c. You always privilege life in your texts.

H. c. Yes. Yes, that is the dominant. I always come back to it. Whatever may happen, "one cannot not," even in the very gesture of writing, which by definition is a gesture of retreat. It is a gesture that you make only by retiring, by enclosing yourself, by acting as if you were alone in the world, at least for a while. And what is happening during that time? You write and make an extremely bizarre and relatively autoerotic gesture while the others are behind closed doors and wait until you are done. Nothing, of course, prohibits them from writing also. You see, each person is in his or her corner. I say this laughingly. On the other hand, what I can also say from experience is that writing is—and one cannot deny this—a consolation, happiness in unhappiness. And if unhappiness is near you, real unhappiness is always much stronger than happiness in unhappiness; if someone near you truly suffers, if someone is sick or if there is a war, you do not write. And then you see the limits of writing, because technically it is always situated and written in the present. It is really atemporal. That is why I say it always anticipates other times. When there is no tomorrow, when today is put to fire and the sword, let me say that then, today is stronger than ever. That is when you say that truly unlivable things, the concentration camps, for example, do not have a writing. Another evidence is of course that there is a part of the world that cannot write and that will always only write in silence.

v. c. Like the Third World or, in our context, the Third World women.

h. c. I talked about that in *Vivre l'orange*, which I wrote at the time of the events in Iran. Of course, I went into the streets, I manifested. I did what I could, not being in Iran but in my own skin. These are questions that cannot be solved. These are questions one must ask oneself, and that one must sometimes transform into a dagger, to inflict a good blow on oneself in order not to forget that others suffer. Now, there are also questions of identification. For example, do I identify with Iranian women for reasons of the unconscious? Yes. For reasons of the Orient? Yes. All this traverses my own Arab childhood, if you like. But am I going to identify with Japanese women? No. Of course, I could say that if there were a massacre of Japanese women, I would be in solidarity with them all the time, in the same way that now, in France, one is in solidarity with the Polish "question." Is it true? It is a question. It is true for many and false for many others. I can only do the maximum from where I am by being the most severe judge of my own gestures and my own spending: did I do enough of what I can do from where I am?

So back to the question of the Third World women. I think that I am only a writer, and when I say that, I think that other women are completely militant, some women of the MLF, for example. They struggle for women, for their lives. I do not compare myself with them; I consider that they advance the woman's cause in a much more active and more immediate way than I do. So why, since I think that, do I not do it? I do not do it because it is true that I was born, so to speak, in the skin of writing, and I have writing in the skin. And to live, I need to do what I am doing. So, do I have the right to do it? That is the question. I give myself the right but maybe for the wrong reasons. My need is totally unjustifiable, totally egotistical. I justify myself by saying that there are people who have a calling to write that is strong enough and that our culture is of a type that allows me, for example, to produce what I consider to be a feminine textual breakthrough. I justify myself, but I may be wrong, since I am the one who says it; others may say that this is completely wrong, and I will have committed an enormous historical error.

That is true, but finally I believe in what I do; otherwise, I would not do it. If I were persuaded that what I do is useless, I would not do it. I believe that it is useful, and I think that it can be useful only on the condition that there be a women's movement. If there were no women's movement, I would be prohibited.

V. C. Do you think that the women's movement is caught in a class struggle?

H. C. That is a big question. It is a question which is determined historically. First, in France, no one ignores class struggle. And then, there is always the question of solidarity. But the women's movement in France is not feminist only in the sense of asking for equal rights. When I say that, everybody screams, What do you mean, "only equal rights"? Of course one must demand them. Equalities are needed. But the women's movement does something that is not taken into account by class struggle; that is, it represses or even squashes misogyny. Class struggle reinforces misogyny. It concentrates on social measures and makes fun of women's words, precisely with social measures. And that is perfectly ridiculous; women know it well.

v. c. When one speaks of the "other," does one necessarily refer to a feminine other?

h. c. For reasons of political, historical, and cultural urgency, I am obligated to make distinctions. I would say, for example, if I took my own "little" life, on the level of the anecdote, I would not know whom to designate as my other, my others. I could say that my first others are people of my family. Only if I move now into another, larger sphere, then I produce my other out of a sense of urgency. This other is imposed on me, is dictated in an absolute way to me, by history, by the state of history. Today it is necessarily women, the question of women, the woman. So I have to say, because there is a big distance, that this is not where I started my existence. I would say that it is even for this very reason that the word "other" is an interesting word.

In reality, I impregnate it with love. For me, the other is the other to love. Yet what I may have lived in my existence was that the other had to be hated, feared, that he was the stranger, the foreigner, everything that is bad. I situate the other in what classically or biblically one could have called my neighbor. It is complicated to say this kind of thing. And then you have the whole range of others. For example, I have been working on a text by Lispector that has to do with a bandit, a criminal who has killed many people, a guy one has to get rid of. Little by little, there is an imaginary displacement into the imagination of the other. All of a sudden the bandit emerges, as if there were a kind of invisible line that speaks from one body to another as other, yet as his own other, my other, as a completely foreign other but one whom, precisely, I respect as this other there. That, for me, is absolutely vital, it is for me the supreme value. To respect strangeness, otherness, does not mean that I relegate him to incomprehensibility; on the contrary, I seek to catch the most of what is going to remain preciously incomprehensible for me and that I will in any case never understand, but that I like, that I can admit, that I can tolerate, because really there is always a mystery of the other. In general, when there is a mystery, one feels hostility. One wants to destroy, one wants to oppose it. That is where I think there is an enigmatic kernel of the other that must be absolutely preserved.

v. c. In that case, the other is not sexually determined. It could be any "other."

h. c. It is always anybody.

v. c. But there has been so much talk about the Other-as-woman, often spelled with a capital O.

h. c. When one speaks about the Other-as-woman, what does one mean? I am asking you the question.

Besides, I wonder—when one speaks about the Other-as-woman, one insists on the fact that the other may be any other. What the classical, ordinary, heterosexual woman cannot do is to think of the other woman, for the good reason that she is not the object of her interest, since the object of her interest is man. I do not like the notion "fellow creature," which comes back to the same, which is in any case the elimination of the other and death. As I said, I do not believe in the opposition between men and women. I only believe that one finds a feminine economy in some women, like Eve. You see, God is the name of the law, the name of punishment, of the masculine figure who cannot let himself act in a way that would make people stop at a stage of *jouissance,* of pleasure, simply because otherwise there would be no society, no capitalism, no power struggle; there would not be that which has become our civilization; all this is completely banal. So now, when you take another example, everybody knows it, I mean everybody who has a sense of language obscurely knows it and exploits it in different ways. And everyone obviously does not say what I say. But everyone knows that the law is only the name of the law. So let us take for example Kafka's text, "Before the Law," about which I already spoke in *La Jeune Née*, because it was exemplary for me; I read it in the same mode. You know the story of the peasant who comes from the countryside, from paradise, naively telling himself, I want to go in. Now, that is not the nature of man in general. And, of course, he is told: "No." And you know how he dies, you know the story. What interests me is the manner in which Kafka wrote it. He starts with a title, "Before the Law." Then he starts the first sentence, "Before the law, there is a keeper, the keeper of the door." The man from the country arrives, and you go on, you read everything. Afterward, you ask questions, all the questions that Kafka asked himself in *The Trial,* and you can do, if you like, the interminable exegesis of the admirable story. Except, in fact, what *did* happen? It so happened that there was the first sentence, which starts with "Before the law," and that you, since you are a good, obedient student, do not ask questions; that is to say, you were told "before the law," so all right, you are also before the law and you are there with the country man, asking yourself: May I go in? And what is the law? etc. When the first sentence was already the one that implicated you in the world of law, which is nothing but the utterance of the words "before the law," and right away you start to think that there also is a "behind the law." Simply because it is written, and that is the force of the "it is written." Law is nothing but that, it is empty. It is nothing.

* * *

v. c. What about separation in relation to a word wound?

h. c. I say in a way that is, as a question of extreme violence, banal and not banal—and when I say "I," it is greater than the self—that most women feel this violence of the word, of speech, the violence of verbalization, since speech in effect separates, interrupts something of the lived immediacy. This is normal, necessary, and in certain ways good; yet in others, it is not. It all goes back to history and to the story of the apple. When the name of the apple begins to thicken and replace the apple, we all know that moment, the linguists as well as the psychoanalysts. In women's daily life, this is a big question. The ideal, or the dream, would be to arrive at a language that heals as much as it separates. Could one imagine a language sufficiently transparent, sufficiently supple, intense, faithful so that there would be reparation and not only separation? I am attempting to write in that direction. I try to write on the side of a language as musical as possible.

v. c. A language that sings, words that are sung, traverse the body. What would be the relationship between a musical language and the body?

h. c. There are various levels of relationship between body and language. I think that many people speak a language that has no rapport with the body. Instead of letting emerge from their body something that is carried by voice, by rhythm, and that would be truly inspired, they are before language as before an electric panel. They choose the hypercoded, where nothing traverses. But I think, and everybody knows, that there are other possibilities of language, that are precisely *languages*. That is why I always privilege the ear over the eye. I am always trying to write with my eyes closed. What is going to write itself comes from long before me, *me* [*moi*] being nothing but the bodily medium which formalizes and transcribes that which is dictated to me, that which expresses itself, that which vibrates in almost musical fashion in me and which I annotate with what is not the musical note, which would of course be the ideal. This is not to say that I am opposed to meaning, not at all, but I prefer to speak in terms of poetry. I prefer to say that I am a poet even if I do not write poems, because the phonic and oral dimensions of language are present in poetry, whereas in the banal, clichéd language, one is far removed from oral language.

v. c. You have often defined the kind of writing that you have practiced over the past few years as *écriture féminine*, or more recently, with added caution, as a writing said to be feminine. This writing, poetic and musical, nevertheless engages in dialogue with the major discourses of our times.

h. c. I am obviously not without a minimum of philosophical and analytical knowledge, simply because I am part of a historical period. I cannot act as if I were not a contemporary of myself. Neither do I think that I must wage a mortal war against a certain type of discourse. Like most women of my generation, I believe, I had inhibitions, faced with the rigid, defining, and decisive side of most theoretical discourses. True, I did have resistances. I had to work through them in order to be able to approach the spaces containing a certain amount of useful and necessary knowledge in order to carry out another type of work which would be on the side of femininity. I am not and do not feel like being ignorant. Neither do I feel like being a prisoner of masculine culture, and I do not feel enslaved or threatened by that culture. I retain the open-ended part, that which is not specifically phallocentric, or phallogocentric, as Derrida would say. For example, I have an absolute need—and I must say that at this moment all human beings have a need—not to disregard the unconscious. It is not because it is a man who discovered it that I am going to be afraid it will be a bearded unconscious. Women have not made discoveries, because they have been kept from the scene—absolutely. They have been kept from making discoveries; that must be changed. But that which has been discovered is valid for the universe. I do have knowledge of theoretical discourses. Yet the part that represses women is a part which I quickly learned to detect and from which I keep my distance. One leaves these parts aside. One keeps all that is vital: for example, that which in Freudian discourse describes the trajectory of sexual formation, of drives, of dream work, etc.

v. c. Other theoreticians have defined the notion of writing. How do you see the relationship between what you call *l'écriture dite féminine* and other writings, for example, Derrida's *écriture?*

H. C. I have insisted on the necessity of not taking the classical feminist position, which consists in referring everything back to women and pretending that we have fallen from the sky. As far as women are concerned, some groundbreaking work has been done on the question of difference, on the differential, by Derrida. We know and use his work. The only thing is, of course, that he does not pretend to discuss femininity from the point of view of women. He does not. Yet what he does trace, in the most faithful and lucid manner in all of his texts, is a philosophical problem of sexuality. I would not say of masculine sexuality (that does not mean anything) but of a libidinal economy that really is on the side of masculinity—the way one could speak about it in the past—of which on the one hand he is conscious, on the other unconscious, which is also very interesting because obviously he cannot speak of his unconscious. But he is the only philosopher, and that in my opinion is important, who admits that there is a textual unconscious, who at the same time works on the unconscious other—but of course his own unconscious is also at work. When he works on the unconscious in Freud, one can also see his own unconscious appear; that is very important. For us, this is good, it is an essential contribution. So I say, and some do not seem to understand this, he is on the other shore. There is a river and there are riverbanks. It is true that he is, insofar as women are concerned, on the other side, on the side of the masculine territory, and we are on this side. But this common river does not separate—of course not. And if I have recourse to this metaphor, it is deliberately, and it is to say that it is really an aquatic metaphor, that this water is necessary, that it bathes shores and harbors and that one navigates in it. That is how one communicates.

v. c. However, this shore should, at the limit, disappear.

h. c. No, I do not think so. No, precisely, I do not believe that it should. One should not think in terms of making disappear something that does not really separate, something that hyphenates, a water that binds, that organizes a mobile and living continuity. But on the other hand, I believe that one has to work at this geography. One must explore effectively all the minute details, something which generally one does not do. This is where we work.

v. c. And how do you read the well-known and much debated passage from *Spurs,* which I quote from memory, "If style were man, writing would be woman"?

h. c. I do not remember it. In *Spurs,* Derrida nevertheless deals with a femininity fantasized by Nietzsche. There are many relays which have to be taken into account. Besides, I do not deny that this capacity to read Nietzsche—who lets himself be fantasized, or one may say hallucinated, by a phantasm of femininity—does signify a proximity. There is proximity, true, but it is not an identity. What about the phantasm itself? Derrida has very well defined the phantasm of femininity that haunted philosophical discourse, a phantasm which, among women, should provoke laughter. Unless, of course, they take themselves for men.

v. c. You say that it is necessary to "go outside" philosophical discourse.

h. c. Where did I say that?

v. c. In *Illa,* perhaps.

H. C. I would be careful about this statement. I do not know where or whether I wrote it. I am capable, when I speak, of saying things that I would not sign. Because I do distinguish as one should, I think, between speech and writing. For example, I reread when I write, and if I write nonsense, I apologize. In speech, I do not apologize. Like everybody, the spoken word escapes me; I may say things that are incorrect or insufficiently precise. For example, "to go outside of philosophy": I do not know whether I wrote it. If there is a philosophical culture, if one may say so, it would be the culture in which the philosophers are enclosed. Who must go outside of philosophy? I do not know if women are the ones. I am not sure about that at all. One should see in what context this formulation occurs and ask whether we women are in it. In order to go outside of it, one has to be in it. I am not sure that we are in philosophy. Must I answer directly? I do not believe that the question is that specific. For example, am I in philosophy? I do not think so. I have a relationship to philosophy, but it is one of dialogue, and I know very well that I am not a philosopher. In other words, I do not have a philosophical calling. I do not answer the calling of philosophy even if I am in a duet with something "philosophical," yet all the while invoking all the liberties warranted or unwarranted of poetry. Insofar as philosophy is concerned, if I refer myself especially to Derrida, it is because he, of course, works on excess. How to exceed, not how to exit from, how to go out of, and one exceeds without forgetting or retracting.

v. c. He says that writing is always based on an originary repression, whereas you write of undoing repressions.

H. C. I do not think that I am in disagreement with him. I suppose that when he says that, he says it in relation to writing, any kind of writing, any kind of inscription, philosophical, poetic, etc. In *Grammatology*, he treats of writing in general, of the text in general. When I talk about writing, that is not what I am talking about. One must displace at that moment; I do not speak about the concept of writing the way Derrida analyzes it. I speak in a more idealistic fashion. I allow this to myself; I disenfranchise myself from the philosophical obligations and corrections, which does not mean that I disregard them. I do not believe in a complete undoing of repressions. We are made of repressions, and the unconscious is nothing but that. However, one may attempt to write as closely as possible to the unconscious, to the area of repressions.

Yes, and also I want to write as freely as possible. Philosophical discourse, if you like, is not free, since it must obey imperatives of signification. A philosopher is obligated to hold on to logic—even Derrida, for example, who pushes his work to the limit where logic vacillates. Even when, or precisely when, he situates himself in the undecidable, that is to say where nothing cuts, decides, where everything is unhinged, where everything permanently vacillates. This is also recuperated and must again obey a new law, that of the logic of non-logic, because the moment you name the undecidable, you already, in a certain way, arrest it. Derrida knows this. That is why he always says that each time he arrests, each time he coins a concept, he hurries to put it into that general movement of oscillation in order not to make of it a master concept. But it is like a ford of a river, if you like: he must jump from concept to concept, or from rock to rock, whereas I allow myself to say, since I do not have any obligation toward philosophy, I really do prefer swimming. I prefer being in the water and openly in the water; for me, those inscriptions with which Derrida must deal do not exist. He says it himself.

For example, look at the way I write, how I write, how I reread myself. When a philosopher rereads himself, I do not know how he does it. I suppose that his reading is on the side of an economy, of signification, of its force. He wants to transmit as much meaning as possible. That is the writing of Derrida, who condenses in a way that is a polysemy. He transmits an intensity, a richness of condensation, of meaning. Philosophy is demonstrative. When I reread my texts, I do not seek to demonstrate. One could even accuse me of it. I do not ignore Derrida's philosophical work, in the wake of Heidegger, on presence, essence, all that you quoted me. If I were a philosopher, I could never allow myself to speak in terms of presence, essence, etc., or of the meaning of something. I would be capable of carrying on a philosophical discourse, but I do not. I let myself be carried off by the poetic word. Is it a mad word? Does it say something? I must say that my steed or my barge and my poetic body never do forget the philosophical rigor. So what is happening? Philosophy is like an accompaniment, but humorous. If one knows how to read and has a knowledge of philosophy, one will see that there is something like a surreptitious echo in everything I say, when I say that I believe in presence, in the coming onto presence. I know the Heideggerian problematic, which I have read very closely and which impassions me, but I have no obligation toward that kind of thinking, toward this kind of rigor. I take it into account but precisely as that from which I can take my distance. And I would even say that it is my mission, my calling, to be able to distance myself from it.

In my seminar, we work on texts by Heidegger and Derrida. We have also worked, for example, on texts by Rilke while traversing the Heideggerian field, or the Rilko-Heideggerian field. I do not have to produce theory. Like Rilke—he did not have to produce theory. Heidegger did that for him. Rilke, with the peculiar instrument infinitely freer than philosophical discourse, produced a series of works that are living objects in which you see, for example, how a rose opens up. In a certain way, poetry is disenfranchised from the obligation that philosophy has: to demonstrate, justify.

v. c. It seems that you make the same distinction between writer and philosopher as between woman and man.

h. c. Yes, of course. The closest allies of us women are the poets. They are our friends. True, they are the ones who are the furthest removed from anything decisive, cutting, and they let their femininity traverse them.

v. c. Do you read as writer or as critic?

H. C. I do my own reading. I am not looking to evaluate a text, or to theorize about it. Of course, I can do it, and sometimes I do it. For example, earlier in my life, under different circumstances, when I used to teach for the *agrégation*. But it is not at all my wish or my desire. I do not care to master a text. I am not interested in that. I am not interested in making it enter into categories, because really I grant myself the luxury to read in texts only that which for me is a question of life and death. So when I read, I ask of the text questions that I ask of myself. I ask questions like "where does it come from?" Questions of origin. Where does it go? How far? What stops? What arrests? My questions are of, and concern, human beings. That is what I focus on in my seminars. I ask questions concerning human beings in general. What causes some people to waste their lives, not to know how to live, and what makes others capable of pushing back the limits of death in life? And I ask myself questions concerning love in relation to a life-giving body or to one that gives death. Last year in my seminar I worked on two kinds of knowledge. At another time I took into consideration what I call fundamental traces, in the work of Kafka, Lispector, and Blanchot, for example. When one reads a text, one is able to see deep and profound tracings that are not themes—that are questions, you understand, not themes; themes are something else. I am talking of questions that are the very root of the works. What I took as root, as motive, of Kafka's work were a series of disturbing propositions from a notebook for *Preparation of a Wedding in the Country,* in which Kafka, in one of these internal dialogues where he constantly divides himself against himself, ends up by saying, "One can, however, not not live." He asks the question of the faith, what is faith, is there a faith, faiths, and he arrives at this proposition. There is all of Kafka. It is his way of living, of remaining in life, alive, in order not to give in to death. It is all in this sentence: "*Man kann doch nicht, nicht leben.*" You have *kann,* you have *leben,* one can live, but it is not true, one has *nicht, nicht.* That is to say that at the heart of existence is that double negation, "one can not, not." And eventually, one sees precisely his economy. It is an economy of resistance, of resistance to death and not of affirmation of life.

If you follow this level of tragic, tormented depth, you will find by the same journey, by the same itinerary, at similar crossroads, Clarice Lispector, who arrives from the opposite side with her body, her torments, with her life, with her sorrows, and she says that to live is sufficient. I need nothing else but to live; living produces living. She does not say, "not not," she says the opposite. She affirms life in a pure affirmation; that is "feminine," that is the source itself, whereas in Kafka you will find the source cut off, cut off all the time. Continuity in Lispector, cuts in Kafka. These are two structures that are specifically "feminine" and "masculine," if you like. Though let me remind you that I do not equate *feminine* with woman and *masculine* with man. To say that which it would be interesting to be able to say, one would have to change the words. However, it is true that Lispector does not say "no, no." She is a woman who says things as closely as possible to a feminine economy, that is to say, one of the greatest generosity possible, of the greatest virtue, of the greatest spending. When I say that, it is because there is a common trait between her and Kafka. Their bodies paid for the difficulty of being on the side of writing in an absolutely similar way. I do not mean that I am not reading "literary objects," but I want to consider in them traces of life, enigmatic accounts.

So, if you like, living beings are for me to be read in a similar way, as closely and as passionately as possible. Simply, I do not talk about them, because they are alive, and so I would be afraid to do so. I respect, but I do not say—except in intimacy, of course—what I can discover, guess, that is mysterious in such and such a person, for example. And people, my students, do give themselves to read.

v. c. The oneiric elements seem to be of great importance in your texts. You constantly write about dreams, from dreams.

H. c. Immense. It is funny. I can tell you my love story with dreams. In a certain way I am a dreamer. So it is very complicated. I owe everything, almost everything to dream. What does that mean? It means that there is somebody else besides me, of course. I owe everything to somebody else, and in my innocence of times past, I felt guilty because when I started to write I wrote under pressure, under dictation, under the influence of the dream, which made me terribly ashamed. I was not the one who was writing. When I say I write during the day, that is to say that during the day I annotate, like a secretary of my unconscious. I note all that which inscribes itself, produces itself, develops at night, and which is infinitely larger than I. I used to be ashamed of it, I thought it was a kind of superpassion, because it happened at night. During the day I was there, because somebody had spoken. I was like somebody absolutely archaic. I had very primitive fears. I said to myself, what if all that would become silent or if it would not come back? I would not write anymore. I did not dare to say it. Now, it makes me laugh. Because after all, I know a little more on the account of the unconscious. It is like the sea, it is interminable. When it is silent, it also speaks. There are periods of desert. These are warning signs, exactly as in life.

Now I know about this. I know that if I am cut off from dreams, that means that there is a cut in communication with the deepest, the most essential life, with others in myself, because I let myself be alienated by numerous exterior and superficial activities. It can happen. At that moment one does not write. It is a bad thing. It is a betrayal of the deepest elements in one's relationship with the unconscious. The unconscious, as we know it, does not lie. So when I cannot write, that means that I am lying in my inner depth.

V. C. You also seem to privilege myths, which are closely related to dreams.

H. C. I work a lot on the level of myths, as much as on that of dreams. In reality, myth was that which took the place of analysis in former times. The myth of Oedipus, not at all in a Freudian mode, was of great importance. It showed that there was the universe, but one knew that there was also something else. One knew that something stronger than the social existed. I am passionately interested in myths, because they are always (this is well known) outside the law, like the unconscious. Only afterward there is the story, which signifies that there has been a clash between the in-law and the outlaw. I do not say transgression, because it is *not* transgressive. The other world comes and collides with reality, with the reality principle. What happens? Interpretation, of course, because we do have myths and their interpretations. One never questions enough the traditions of interpretation of myth, and all myths have been referred to a masculine interpretation. If we women read them, we read them otherwise. That is why I often nourish my texts, in my own way, at those mythic sources.

v. c. In everything you write, you are also very close to analysis. What do you think of castration?

H. c. I think that castration is fundamental, unfortunately. One has to speak of castration as a phantasm, a fear. True, men are built, or rather one builds masculinity, virility, from one's own resistance to castration. I think that most men are obligated by it. I am not sure if there are many men who are protected from castration, from this kind of rite which of course is the passage through the moment that Freud describes very well with his story of the Medusa, the moment when there is erection, as rite, in the scene of castration. I believe that it structures the economy of men, but what does it give us women? Are we protected from castration? I think that there are women who are completely protected from the world which is organized around the resistance to castration. Surely, there are some. I believe that I know some. Yet since it is a phantasm, it may be communicated. There are women who are under the spell of castration, who are taken in by a phallocratic space. For them, the rite is something hallucinated, since it cannot rely on a bodily inscription, since there is no corporeal representation. Men experience pain in being castrated, yet castration is something imaginary that one feels very vividly, very strongly. I think that women have an analogous situation to that of men. They can feel a kind of castration, a feminine castration. Maybe the word should be displaced. But it should be displaced from a "masculine" border, a little like "masculine" and "feminine." The problem is that on the one hand, for the man there is an anatomic origin of the imaginary model, situated there where the little boy has his penis; on the other, his sexuality is probably not as stable, as continuous, as the feminine sexuality of *jouissance*, of pleasure, which is organized by an absence of cuts.

V. C. On the level of anatomy?

H. C. Of anatomy, on the level of the organ, no. But in the way of pleasure. That is where something could be transformed.

V. C. Do you think that your mode of writing is able to transform, to change the situation of women? Is there a strategic value?

H. C. I do not know whether I can effectuate transformations. But one always arrives at something when something that has been silenced is expressed, when something that has been inhibited expresses itself. It is true that it liberates something.

V. C. Do you consider your writing to be an action?

H. C. Yes, I think so. I think that there is also a test of reading. Texts with a strong "femininity," like some—not all—the texts of Lispector, put to test a certain *jouissance*. There are people who resist, who feel it as threat, while others are relieved by this very kind of rhythm.

V. C. When you talk about *jouissance*, are you not talking about something that had contributed to exclude women, to define them from a masculine border?

H. C. No, I do not think so. I do not see how men talk about feminine *jouissance*. That is precisely what devours them. That is what they are talking about in the mode of not-knowing. That is also what the analysts say, that is what Lacan said, when he spoke of women and of their pleasures: "They have nothing to say, they cannot speak." Fine. That means that he cannot hear them. It means also that he does not know anything about it. He says it clearly when he says: "All right, if you have something to say, say it." But he thinks that women have nothing to say. That is not true. Of course, they say it otherwise. They can say it. It can be defined. I think that in the classical heterosexual scene, the woman generally obeys the masculine demand, which is to give pleasure in the masculine way, to obey the masculine phantasm of feminine *jouissance,* which would be totally, exclusively genital and which leads to effects of inhibition, frigidity, in women. But a woman who is not deprived of her body must be able to find something of it again, and of course it is up to her to talk about it, to inscribe something of it; it is absolutely not organized in the centralized, ritualized way of men, that is true. But women have to say that, and their best listeners will still be women. I am trying to say a little of it in my texts.

v. c. If women differ from men in their mode of *jouissance,* following your distinctions of feminine and masculine economies, they should also differ in their relation to the gift.

H. c. The question of the gift is a question on which we have worked a lot, marking it and following it, if one may say, with a step as light and as airy, as "feminine" as possible. The question is of course the following: Is it possible that there is a gift? It is a question that has been treated at length by Derrida in a seminar on the philosophical mode, etc. Is there such a thing as a gift; can the gift take place? At the limit, one can ask oneself about the possibility of a real gift, a pure gift, a gift that would not be annulled by what one could call a countergift. That is also what Derrida worked on.

How does one give? It starts in a very simple way: in order for a gift to be, *I* must not be the one to give. A gift has to be like grace, it has to fall from the sky. If there are traces of origin of the *I* give, there is no gift—there is an I-give. Which also signifies: say "thank you," even if the other does not ask you to say it. As soon as we say thank you, we give back part or the whole gift. We have been brought up in the space of the debt, and so we say thank you. Is it possible to imagine that there can be a gift? This presupposes that *I* be in parentheses, that *I* accede to a transparency but without disappearance, because otherwise it would be a divine gift. And one does not receive anything from God. The gift has to be sent in such a way that it does not come back immediately, and it has to arrive at its destination. That is one of Derrida's problematics. Does the gift arrive at its destination? For there to be gift, there has to be reception. Reception has to be equal to donation, there has to be an equal generosity of reception. So a real gift is quite rare.

* * *

v. c. In your own texts, you started from the question of waiting and you come back to the problem of waiting, but now it is displaced. You also critiqued presence, essence, and you now come back to them. How do you see these changes in your positions?

H. c. I am first going to take the question of waiting, because, as a matter of fact, it has been symptomatic of an evolution. I believe that I have dealt with it in former texts; I am sure I must have written about scenes of bad expectations, bad waitings, scenes of impatience. I say that I would be surprised if I had criticized the woman in the scene. Rather I must have criticized the scene itself with its content, cruel, sadistic, with suspense. I may be wrong. I must have at a certain moment spoken of the drama lived by the woman waiting. It is an old drama, it is that which one sees in literature since its origins. It is that which makes man leave the house. He leaves and woman waits; that can be carried extremely far. I would even say that culturally, woman has been assigned to immobility and man to navigation, and that the model is Ulysses and Penelope. Maybe Penelope was the first woman writer, since she spent her time writing and unwriting, precisely so that her man might come back into the space of the book. It is true that in a period that would correspond roughly to classical tragedy, or to the story of any classically heterosexual woman, the story is always the same, Ulysses and Penelope. One would like to see Penelope's tapestry; one does not know what is on it—most likely painful stories of anguish. But that is when waiting is painful, is organized precisely around an absence, around a lack, around the violence of the other, etc.

In my most recent texts, I believe in particular in *With ou l'art de l'innocence,* I work on something entirely different. I work on a happy expectation which could be compared, for example, to that of the pregnant mother, who expects a child, as one says. I find this a wonderful expression. She waits the time it takes for the child to be born. And not only that, but she takes pleasure in waiting, for nine months. It is a wait which is on the side of gestation, of production. I say this metaphorically. I will give you a play on words: *attendre,* to wait, and *hâte tendre,* tender haste. *La tendre hâte,* the tender haste, the insistence on the wait which is tender, which is not violent, which is expected, which is soft, sweet, and not impatient. I do not want to talk about a kind of resigned patience which is the Christian patience—not at all—but about a capacity to live, a creative capacity, which is not obliged to precipitate itself like a *fiat.* It is not that of the woman who waits in a situation of cruelty that is imposed on her, of violence, but on the contrary a wait that is capable of taking pleasure in each instant, that does not jump over instants by saying, I cannot wait until the end of nine months. She enjoys each time, each measure. Clarice Lispector, for example, sings the present, so that each moment, each instant, is a blessing lived to its fullest.

I have to say that there are several conditions for this. First, you cannot be in the painful situation where you are made to wait and where it is you who do the waiting. Waiting is an art, our life has its rhythms, etc. The present times with their precipitation, technologies, accelerated daily rhythms, television, have destroyed in us the "good old time," a human time. As soon as one is in an urban space, one does not have time anymore. Time flies by us, we do not live it. One must leave and retreat. I am only saying the obvious. I think that when one retreats, one is also already so frenetic that one starts to run again when one is by the sea where there are no bus stops, no television screens.

V. C. What about your *cheminement,* your development?

H. C. I think that what is inscribed in what I have written is a certain story, a certain history, which is mine and, I believe, that of every woman. I think it is quite exemplary. Besides, it is truly a history insofar as it has a development in time, because I absolutely do believe in experience. I think that we traverse in time moments which, little by little, allow us to advance and to learn to live. One does not know how to live; one learns to live, in my case traditionally, since I come from a classical milieu. After a while, it is true, something disengages, detaches itself. One could distinguish at the same time large biographical and textual periods that mark the stages in a *cheminement,* which in any case will always be there because at the bottom I am really a questioner. I cannot even imagine that I will get to the end of the questions asked of me in such overabundance. I do not cease not to understand. Simply, the things I do not understand renew themselves incessantly. Once I have understood something that I did not understand before, it is behind me. And I open myself before the next enigma. Then I have something else that is before me, always like a wonderful America to be discovered, but always to be discovered. . . .

Notes

1. Textual Strategies

1 MLF is the acronym of the *Mouvement de libération des femmes* (Women's Liberation Movement). In an interview with Catherine Clément in *La Matin* (July 16, 1980), Antoinette Fouque, one of its founders, explains the genesis of the movement, which grew out of the political scene of May 1968. Women noticed that political contradiction did not deal with sexual contradiction and grouped themselves around a movement called *Psych et po* (Psychoanalysis and Politics). At Paris VIII–Vincennes they studied the only discourse that dealt with sexual difference, psychoanalysis. Reading Freud, Marx, and Lacan, they first had to overcome the resistance from the Sartrian camp. The acronym MLF started to circulate in the early seventies. At the end of 1973, Antoinette Fouque and some other women founded the publishing house Des Femmes. Underlining that their enemy is not *man* but phallocracy, she states that their aim is "to transform women's condition into one not of emancipation but of independence." Discussing the danger of disintegration the movement faces with the progressive institutionalization of woman (laws on abortion, laws on rape, laws on homosexuality, an office of the condition of woman), she explains how the MLF, after establishing a publishing house and founding a monthly and a weekly paper, felt the necessity to create a *legal* movement in 1979.
2 Jacques Derrida, "La Double Séance," in *La Dissémination* (Paris: Seuil, 1972), 71.

2. Beyond a Coincidence of Opposites: The Step of the Gradiva

1 Hélène Cixous, *Prénoms de personne* (Paris: Seuil, 1974), 5. (All Cixous translations are mine.)

2 Ibid.

3 Ibid.

4 Ibid.

5 Cf. Michèle H. Richman, *Reading Georges Bataille* (Baltimore: Johns Hopkins Univ. Press, 1982).

6 Cf. Jean-Joseph Goux, *Freud, Marx: économie et symbolique* (Paris: Seuil, 1973).

7 *Prénoms de personne*, 9.

8 Ibid., 10.

9 Ibid., 15.

10 Ibid., 37.

11 Ibid., 40.

12 Heinrich von Kleist, "Über das Marionettentheater," in *Werke und Briefe*, vol. 3 (Berlin: Aufbau Verlag, 1978), 473–80.

13 *Prénoms de personne*, 301–03.

14 Ibid., 310–11.

15 Hélène Cixous, "The Character of 'Character,' " trans. Keith Cohen, *New Literary History* 5 (Winter 1974), 384–402.

16 See Emile Benvéniste, *Problèmes de linguistique générale*, vol. 1 (Paris: Gallimard, 1966), 322–23, for a discussion of obligation, exchange, and community.

17 Cf. the distinction that Roland Barthes makes in *S/Z*, trans. Richard Miller (New York: Hill and Wang, 1974), 67–69, between character and figure. To say "I," Barthes argues, even without a proper name, is to attribute signifieds to oneself. To say "I" is to give oneself a biographical duration, to give a meaning to time. The figure is different: it is not a legal name, it is an illegal, anachronistic configuration of symbolic relationships. "As figure, the character can oscillate between two roles, without this oscillation having any meaning, for it occurs outside biographical time (outside chronology)."

18 Hélène Cixous, *Le Troisième Corps* (Paris: Grasset, 1970), 13.

19 Jacques Derrida, "La Pharmacie de Platon," in *La Dissémination* (Paris: Seuil, 1972), 146.

20 Jacques Derrida, "From Restricted to General Economy," in *Writing and Difference*, tr. Alan Bass (Chicago: Univ. of Chicago Press, 1978), 251–77, esp. 251–54.

21 Ibid., 261, 263.

22 *Le Troisième Corps*, 21.

23 Ibid., 51.

24 Ibid., 52.

25 Jacques Derrida, *La Voix et le phénomène* (Paris: Presses universitaires de France, 1972), 116 (my translation).

26 *Le Troisième Corps,* 95.

27 Ibid., 96.

28 Ibid.

29 Ibid., 98.

30 Ibid., 106.

31 Ibid., 112.

32 Ibid., 113.

33 Derrida, "La Pharmacie de Platon," 91.

34 *Le Troisième Corps,* 165.

35 Hélène Cixous, *Les Commencements* (Paris: Grasset, 1970), 51.

36 Cf. Jacques Lacan, *Les Quatre Concepts fondamentaux de la psychanalyse* (Paris: Seuil, 1973).

37 *Les Commencements,* 53.

38 Ibid., 83.

39 Ibid., 84.

40 Jacques Derrida, "La Dissémination," in *La Dissémination,* 395 (my translation).

41 Hélène Cixous, *Neutre* (Paris: Grasset, 1972), 19.

42 Ibid., 19.

43 Ibid., 21–22.

44 Ibid., 117.

45 Hélène Cixous, *Portrait du soleil* (Paris: Denoël, 1973), 195.

46 Ibid., 5.

47 Ibid.

48 Ibid., 6.

49 Ibid.

50 Ibid., 11.

51 Ibid., 12.

52 Ibid., 13.

53 Ibid., 54.

54 Ibid., 55.

55 Ibid., 102.

56 Ibid., 132.

57 W. Jensen, "Gradiva," in *Délire et rêves dans la "Gradiva" de Jensen* (Paris: Gallimard, 1949), 122.

58 *Portrait du Soleil,* 121. For a slight rewriting of this paragraph, see Hél-

ène Cixous, *Portrait de Dora* (Paris: Des Femmes, 1976), 105.

59 For recent discussions of the status of the letter in psychoanalysis, see Jacques Lacan, "L'Instance de la lettre dans l'inconscient ou la raison depuis Freud," in *Ecrits* (Paris: Seuil, 1966), 493–528; Serge Leclaire, *Psychanalyser* (Paris: Seuil, 1968).

60 Hélène Cixous, *Partie* (Paris: Des Femmes, 1976), 38. This fragment of *Partie* first appeared appropriately in *La Nouvelle Revue de psychanalyse* 7 (Spring 1973), 335–50.

61 Jacques Derrida, *Glas* (Paris: Galilée, 1974), 7 (my translation).

62 *Partie*, 38.

3. *Writing the Missexual: A Cleopatrician in Her Own Right*

1 Hélène Cixous, *LA* (Paris: Gallimard, 1976), 272.

2 FNAC: an enormous Parisian discount bookstore.

3 Hubert Damisch, "La Culture de poche," reprinted from *Mercure de France* (November 1964): 482–98, in *Ruptures cultures* (Paris: Minuit, 1976), 66 (my translation).

4 Hélène Cixous and Catherine Clément, *La Jeune Née* (Paris: Union Générale d'Editions, 1975), 38.

5 Ibid., 78.

6 Ibid., 230.

7 Ibid., 115–16.

8 Ibid., 126.

9 Ibid., 151.

10 Ibid., 148.

11 Sigmund Freud, "Trieb and Triebschicksale," in *Gesammelte Werke*, vol. 10 (London: Imago, 1918), 214 (my translation).

12 We are following Samuel Weber's discussion of drive in relation to representation in "Der Gesperrte Abort," in *Rückkehr zu Freud* (Frankfurt: Ullstein, 1978), 62–63.

13 Freud, "Trieb und Triebschicksale," 214.

14 Freud, "Das Unbewusste," in Gesammelte Werke, vol. 10, 275–76.

15 *La Jeune Née*, 152.

16 Ibid., 153.

17 Ibid., 154.

18 Cf. Sarah Kofman, *Nietzsche et la métaphore* (Paris: Payot, 1972).

19 Cf. Sarah Kofman, *L'Enigme de la femme dans les textes de Freud* (Paris: Galilée, 1980).

20 *La Jeune Née*, 158.

21 Ibid., 171.

22 Ibid.

23 Cf. Jacques Derrida, "Qual Quelle," in *Marges de la philosophie* (Paris: Minuit, 1972), 325–63.

24 *La Jeune Née*, 172–73.

25 Ibid., 180.

26 Ibid., 212.

27 Ibid., 222.

28 Ibid., 226.

29 *Prénoms de personne*, 140.

30 Luce Irigaray, "The Blind Spot of an Old Dream of Symmetry," in *Spéculum de l'autre femme* (Paris: Minuit, 1974), 7–161 (my translation of the title).

31 *La Jeune Née*, 237.

32 Ibid., 238–39.

33 E.g., cf. Gerald Graff's reaction to my reading of Cixous in *Literature against Itself* (Chicago: Univ. of Chicago Press, 1979), 80–82.

34 *La Jeune Née*, 178.

35 *LA*, 243.

36 Ibid.

37 *Partie*, 16.

38 Jacques Derrida, "Entre crochets," *Digraphe* 8 (1976): 105 (my translation).

39 Ibid., 106.

40 Phyllis Chesler, *Women and Madness* (Paris: Payot, 1975). I return to the American title.

41 *Poétique* 26 (1976): 129.

42 Ibid., 131.

43 Ibid., 241.

44 Ibid., 247.

45 Ibid., 244.

46 For another reading of the artificiality of margarine, see Jean-Claude Lebensztejn, "Photorealism, Kitsch and Venturi," Trans. Kate Cooper. *Sub-stance* 31 (1982): 75–77.

47 Jacques Derrida, "+R (par-dessus le marché)," *Derrière le miroir* 214 (May 1975).

48 Derrida, *Glas*, 46 (my translation).

49 T. J. Kline, "Orpheus Transcending: Bertolucci's 'Last Tango in Paris,'"

International Review of Psychoanalysis 3 (1975): 85–95.

50 Hélène Cixous, "La Missexualité, où jouis-je?" *Poétique* 26 (1976): 248.

51 *LA*, 110.

52 Sigmund Freud, "Über die Weibliche Sexualität," in *Gesammelte Werke*, vol. 14 (London: Imago, 1933).

53 *LA*, 141.

54 Hélène Cixous, Annie Leclerc, and Madeleine Gagnon, *La Venue à l'écriture* (Paris: Union Générale d'Editions, 1977), 56.

55 Hélène Cixous, *Souffles* (Paris: Des Femmes, 1975), 9.

56 *La Venue à l'ecriture*, 58.

57 *The Exile of James Joyce or the Art of Replacement*, trans. Sally Purcell (New York: David Lewis, 1972), 743, 744.

58 Jacques Derrida, *Of Grammatology*, trans. Gayatri Spivak (Baltimore: Johns Hopkins Univ. Press, 1976), 139–40.

59 *LA*, 219.

60 Ibid., 219–20.

61 Derrida, *Glas*, 161.

62 Ibid., 165.

63 Ibid., 166.

64 For a discussion of the function of Antigone as limit, see Geoffrey Hartman, *Saving the Text* (Baltimore: Johns Hopkins Univ. Press, 1981), 89–90.

65 Derrida, *Glas*, 168.

66 Ibid., 182.

67 *LA*, 7.

68 Ibid., 272.

69 Ibid.

70 Derrida, *Glas*, 288.

71 Hélène Cixous *Angst* (Paris: Des Femmes, 1977), 85.

72 Ibid., 283–84.

4. Accord Koré to Cordelia

1 Jacques Derrida, "Economimesis," in *Mimesis désarticulations* (Paris: Aubier-Flammarion, 1975), 69–70 (my translation).

2 Ibid., 71–72.

3 Ibid., 85. For a discussion of the same passage in relation to the sublime,

see Derrida's "Parergon," in *La Verité en peinture*. (Paris: Flammarion, 1978), 147.

4 Hélène Cixous, *Vivre l'orange* (Paris: Des Femmes, 1980), 79.

5 For a similar reading from a "masculine" border, see Jacques Derrida, "Living On," trans. James Hulbert, in Geoffrey H. Hartman, ed., *Deconstruction and Criticism* (New York: Continuum, 1979), 75–176.

6 Rainer Maria Rilke, *Sonnets to Orpheus*, trans. M. D. Herter Norton (New York: Norton, 1962), 94–95. "Sei immer tot in Eurydike—, singender steige, / preisender steige zurück in den reinen Bezug. / Hier, unter Schwindenden, sei, im Reiche der Neige, / sei ein klingendes Glas, das sich im Klang schon zerschlug." (Be ever dead in Eurydice—, mount more singingly, / mount more praisingly back into the pure relation. / Here, among the waning, be, in the realm of decline, / be a ringing glass that shivers even as it rings.)

7 Hélène Cixous, "L'Approche de Clarice Lispector," *Poétique* 40 (1979): 408–19. Cixous reads Lispector's writing as one of the instant-of-presence, never to be arrested, as in this quotation from *Agua Viva:* "Try to hear what I paint and what I write now. I am going to explain: in painting as in writing I am trying to see only at the moment I see—and not to see through the memory of having seen in a past instant. The instant is this one. The instant is of an imminence that takes my breath away. The instant is, in itself, imminent. At the same time I live it, I throw myself at its passage toward another instant" (p. 414). Let us note that Cixous works on the signified in Lispector; a play on the signifier may have been lost in translation.

8 Ibid., 409.

9 A possible allusion to Jacques Derrida's "Cartouches," in *La Vérité en peinture*, 212–90.

10 Cf. Cixous's title *Un K. Incompréhensible: Pierre Goldman* (Paris: Christian Bourgois, 1975) in defense of the latter's being accused of murder.

11 *Vivre l'orange*, 13.

12 *Portrait du soleil*, 5.

13 *Vivre l'orange*, 55.

14 Hélène Cixous, *Illa* (Paris: Des Femmes, 1980), 156.

15 Ibid., 47.

16 Ibid., 73.

17 Ibid., 46–48.

18 Martin Heidegger, "Souvenir," trans. into French by Jean Launay, in *Approche de Hölderlin* (Paris: Gallimard, 1973), 156–57.

19 *Vivre l'orange*, p. 109.

20 Martin Heidegger, "La Chose," trans. into French by André Préau, in *Essais et conférences* (Paris: Gallimard, 1958), 194–218.

21 *Illa*, 7.

22 Ibid., 8.

23 Ibid., 9.

24 Ibid.

25 Jacques Derrida, *Spurs/Eperons*, trans. Barbara Harlow (Chicago: Univ. of Chicago Press, 1979), 110.

26 *Illa*, 11.

27 Ibid., 11–12.

28 Heidegger, "Souvenir," 156–57. *Muot* is an old word from which *Gemüt* (heart) derives.

29 *Illa*, 21.

30 Ibid., 23.

31 Jacques Derrida, "Pas," *Gramma* 3/4 (1976): 111–216.

32 *Illa*, 129.

33 Ibid., 133.

34 Ibid., 137.

35 Ibid., 208.

36 Ibid., 206.

37 Hélène Cixous, *With ou l'art de l'innocence* (Paris: Des Femmes, 1981), 200.

38 Ibid.

39 Ibid.

40 Ibid., 201.

41 Hélène Cixous, *Limonade tout était si infini* (Paris: Des Femmes, 1982), 264.

42 Hélène Cixous, "12 Août 1980," *Boundary* 2 12 (Summer 1984), forthcoming.

43 Ibid.

44 Ibid.

5. Toward a Promethean *"Féminin Futur"*

1 Hélène Cixous, "Tancrède continue," *Etudes freudiennes* 21.22 (1983): 115.

2 Ibid.

3 Ibid.

4 Hélène Cixous, "Cahier de métamorphoses, *Corps écrit* 6 (1983): 73.

5 Ibid., 75.

Appendix: An Exchange with Hélène Cixous

1 This conversation took place in January 1982. The translation from the French is mine.

Bibliography

Published Works of Hélène Cixous

Cixous, Hélène. *Le Prénom de Dieu*. Paris: Grasset, 1967.
_____. *L'Exil de James Joyce ou l'art du remplacement*. Paris: Grasset, 1968.
_____. *Dedans*. Paris: Grasset, 1969.
_____. *Les Commencements*. Paris: Grasset, 1970.
_____. *Le Troisième Corps*. Paris: Grasset, 1970.
_____. *Un Vrai Jardin*. Paris: Editions de l'Herne, 1971.
_____. *Neutre*. Paris: Grasset, 1972.
_____. *La Pupille*. Paris: Cahiers Renaud-Barrault, 1972.
_____. *Portrait du soleil*. Paris: Denoël, Collection Les Lettres Nouvelles, 1973.
_____. *Tombe*. Paris: Seuil, 1973.
_____. *Prénoms de personne*. Paris: Seuil, Collection Poétique, 1974.
_____. *La Jeune Née* (en collaboration avec Catherine Clément). Paris: Union Générale d'Éditions, Collection "10/18," 1975.
_____. *Un K. incompréhensible: Pierre Goldman*. Paris: Christian Bourgois, 1975.
_____. *Révolutions pour plus d'un Faust*. Paris: Seuil, 1975.
_____. "Le Rire de la Méduse." *L'Arc* (1975): 39–54.
_____. *Souffles*. Paris: Des Femmes, 1975.
_____. *LA*. Paris: Gallimard, 1976.
_____. "La Missexualité, où jouis-je?" *Poétique* 26 (1976): 240–49.
_____. *Partie*. Paris: Des Femmes, 1976.
_____. *Portrait de Dora*. Paris: Des Femmes, 1976.
_____. *Angst*. Paris: Des Femmes, 1977.
_____. *La Venue à l'écriture* (en collaboration avec Annie Leclerc et

Madeleine Gagnon). Paris: Union Générale d'Éditions, Collection "10/18," 1977.

———. *Chant du corps interdit, le nom d'Oedipe.* Paris: Des Femmes, 1978.

———. *Préparatifs de noces au-delà de l'abîme.* Paris: Des Femmes, 1978.

———. *Ananké.* Paris: Des Femmes, 1979.

———. "L'Approche de Clarice Lispector." *Poétique* 40 (1979): 408–19.

———. *Vivre l'orange.* Bilingual edition, trans. Ann Liddle and Sarah Cornell. Paris: Des Femmes, 1979.

———. *Illa.* Paris: Des Femmes, 1980.

———. *With ou l'art de l'innocence.* Paris: Des Femmes, 1981.

———. *Limonade tout était si infini.* Paris: Des Femmes, 1982.

———. "Cahier de métamorphoses." *Corps écrit* 6 (1983): 65–7

———. "Tancrède continue." *Etudes freudiennes* 21.22 (1983): 115–31.

———. "12 Août 1980." Bilingual edition, trans. Betsy Wing. *Boundary* 2 12 (Summer 1984).

Translations of Hélène Cixous

Cixous, Hélène. *The Exile of James Joyce or the Art of Replacement.* Translated by Sally Purcell. New York: David Lewis, 1972.

———. "The Character of 'Character.'" Translated by Keith Cohen. *New Literary History* 5 (Winter 1974): 384–402.

———. "At Circe's, or the Self-Opener." Translated by Carol Bové. *Boundary* 2 3 (Winter 1975): 387–97.

———. Interview with Christiane Makward. *Sub-stance* 13 (1976): 19–37.

———. "The Laugh of the Medusa." Translated by Keith Cohen and Paula Cohen. *Signs* 1 (Summer 1976): 875–99.

———. *La Jeune Née* (en collaboration avec Catherine Clément). Translated by Betsy Wing. Minneapolis: Univ. of Minnesota Press. Forthcoming.

———. Special number of *Boundary* 2 12 (Summer 1984). Edited by Verena Andermatt-Conley. Forthcoming.

Critical Studies of Hélène Cixous

Cameron, Beatrice. "Letter to Cixous." *Sub-stance* 17 (1977): 159–65.

Conley, Verena Andermatt. "Missexual Misstery." *Diacritics* 7 (Summer 1977): 70–82.

_____. "Writing the Letter: the lower-case of hélène cixous." *Visible Language* 12 (Summer 1978): 305–18.

_____. "Cixous and the Uncovery of a Feminine Language." *Women and Literature* 7 (Winter 1979): 38–48.

Duren, Brian. "Cixous' Exorbitant Texts." *Sub-stance* 32 (1981): 26–38.

Evans, Martha Noel. "Portrait of Dora: Freud's Case History as Reviewed by Hélène Cixous." *Sub-stance* 36 (1982): 64–71.

Finas, Lucette. "Le pourpre du neutre." In *Le Bruit d'Iris*. Paris: Flammarion, 1981.

Gibbs, Anna. "Cixous and Gertrude Stein." *Meanjin* 38 (1979): 281–93.

Jones, Ann Rosalind. "Writing the Body: Toward an Understanding of *L'Ecriture féminine*." *French Studies* 7 (1981): 247–63.

Kuhn, Annette. "Introduction to Hélène Cixous's 'Castration or Decapitation?'" *Signs* 7 (1981): 36–40.

Makward, Christiane. "Structures du silence ou délire: Marguerite Duras, Hélène Cixous." *Poétique* 9 (1978): 314–24.

Marks, Elaine, and Isabelle de Courtivron, eds. *New French Feminisms*. Amherst: Univ. of Massachusetts Press, 1980.

Micha, René. "La Tête de Dora sous Cixous. *Critique* 33 (1977): 114–21.

Richman, Michèle. "Sex and Signs: The Language of French Feminist Criticism." *Language and Style* 1980, 62–80.

Stanton, Donna C. "Language and Revolution: The Franco-American Disconnection." In *The Future of Difference*, edited by Hester Eisenstein and Alice Jardine, 73–87. Boston: Hall, 1980.

Other Works Cited

Barthes, Roland. *S/Z*. 1970. Translated by Richard Miller. New York: Hill and Wang, 1974.

Bataille, Georges. "La Part maudite." *Oeuvres complètes*, vol. 7, 19–179. Paris: Gallimard, 1976.

_____. "L'Histoire de l'érotisme." *Oeuvres complètes*, vol. 8, 9–165. Paris: Gallimard, 1976.

Beauvoir, Simone de. *Le Deuxième Sexe I*. Paris: Gallimard, Collection Idées, 1949.

Benvéniste, Emile. *Problèmes de linguistique générale*. vol. 1. Paris: Gallimard, Collection Bibliothèque des Sciences Humaines, 1966.

Chesler, Phyllis. *Women and Madness*. New York: Avon, 1973. Preface to French ed. by Hélène Cixous. Paris: Payot, Collection Traces, 1975.

Damisch, Hubert. *Ruptures cultures*. Paris: Minuit, Collection Critique, 1976.

Deleuze, Gilles. *Logique du Sens*. Paris: Minuet, 1971.

Derrida, Jacques. *De la Grammatologie*. Paris: Minuit, 1967. Translated by Gayatri Spivak under the title *Of Grammatology*. Baltimore: Johns Hopkins Univ. Press, 1976.

———. *L'Ecriture et la Différence*. Paris: Seuil, 1967. Translated by Alan Bass under the title *Writing and Difference*. Chicago: Univ. of Chicago Press, 1978.

———. *La Dissémination*. Paris: Seuil, 1972. Translated by Barbara Johnson under the title *Dissemination*. Chicago: Univ. of Chicago Press, 1981.

———. *Marges de la philosophie*. Paris: Minuit, 1972. Translated by Alan Bass under the title *Margins of Philosophy*. Chicago: Univ. of Chicago Press, 1982.

———. *La Voix et le phénomène*. Paris: Presses universitaires de France, Collection Epithémée, 1972. Translated by David B. Allison under the title *Speech and Phenomena*. Evanston, Ill.: Northwestern Univ. Press, 1973.

———. *Glas*. Paris: Galilée, 1974.

———. "Economimesis." In Derrida, Sylviane Agacinski, et al., *Mimesis désarticulations*. Paris: Aubier-Flammarion, 1975.

———. "+R (par-dessus le marché)." *Derrière le miroir* 214 (May 1975).

———. "Entre crochets." *Digraphe* 8 (1976).

———. "Pas." *Gramma* 3/4 (1976): 111–216.

———. *Spurs: Nietzsche's Styles/Eperons: les styles de Nietzsche*. Bilingual edition. Translated by Barbara Harlow. Chicago: Univ. of Chicago Press, 1978.

———. *La Vérité en peinture*. Paris: Flammarion, 1978.

———. "Living On: Border Lines." Translated by James Hulbert. In *Deconstruction and Criticism*, edited by Geoffrey H. Hartman, 75–176. New York: Continuum, 1979.

———. *La Carte postale de Socrate à Freud et au-delà*. Paris: Flammarion, 1980.

Freud, Sigmund. *The Standard Edition of the Complete Psychological*

Works of Sigmund Freud. Edited by James Strachey. 24 vols. London: Hogarth Press, 1953–74. *Gesammelte Werke.* 18 Bände. London: Imago, 1900–40.

Goux, Jean-Joseph. *Freud, Marx: économie et symbolique.* Paris: Seuil, 1973.

Graff, Gerald. *Literature against Itself: Literary Ideas in Modern Society.* Chicago: Univ. of Chicago Press, 1979.

Hartman, Geoffrey H. *Saving the Text.* Baltimore: Johns Hopkins Univ. Press, 1981.

Hegel, G. W. F. *The Phenomenology of Mind.* Translated by J. B. Baillie. New York: Harper Colophon Books, 1967.

Heidegger, Martin. *Essais et conférences.* Translated into French by André Préau. Paris: Gallimard, 1958.

_____. *Approche de Hölderlin.* Translated into French by Henri Corbin, Michel Deguy, François Fedier, and Jean Launay. Paris: Gallimard, 1973.

Hoffman, E. T. A. *The Best Tales of Hoffmann.* Edited by E. F. Bleier. New York: Dover, 1967.

Irigaray, Luce. *Spéculum de l'autre femme.* Paris: Minuit, Collection Critique, 1974.

Jensen, W. "Gradiva." In *Délire et rêves dans la "Gradiva" de Jensen,* translated into French by E. Zak and G. Sadoul, 9–122. Paris: Gallimard, Collection Idées, 1949.

Kleist, Heinrich von. *Das Erdbeben in Chili* and *Die Marquise von O.* In *Sämtliche Werke,* 120–32, 86–119. München: Winkler, 1967.

_____. "Über das Marionettentheater." In *Werke und Briefe,* vol. 3, 473–80. Berlin: Aufbau Verlag, 1978.

Kline, T. J. "Orpheus Transcending: Bertolucci's 'Last Tango in Paris.'" *International Review of Psychoanalysis* 3 (1975): 85–95.

Kofman, Sarah. *Nietzsche et la métaphore.* Paris: Payot, 1972.

_____. *L'Enigme de la femme dans les textes de Freud.* Paris: Galilée, 1980.

Lacan, Jacques. *Ecrits.* Paris: Seuil, Collection Le Champ Freudien, 1966.

_____. *Les Quatre Concepts fondamentaux de la psychanalyse.* Paris: Seuil, 1973.

Leclaire, Serge. *Psychanalyser.* Paris: Seuil, Collection Le Champ Freudien, 1968.

Lebensztejn, Jean-Claude. "Photorealism, Kitsch and Venturi." Translated by Kate Cooper. *Sub-stance* 31 (1982): 75–104.

Lispector, Clarice. *Perto do Coracão Selvagem.* 5th ed. Rio de Janeiro: Livraria José Olympio Editora, 1974. Published in French under the title *Près du coeur sauvage.* Paris: Plon, n.d.

Mauss, Marcel. "Essai sur le don. Forme et raison de l'échange dans les sociétés archaïques." In *Sociologie et Anthropologie,* 145–284. Paris: Presses Universitaires de France, 1950. Translated by Ian Cunnison under the title *The Gift: Forms and Functions of Exchange in Archaic Societies.*

Richman, Michèle H. *Reading Georges Bataille: Beyond the Gift.* Baltimore: Johns Hopkins Univ. Press, 1982.

Rilke, Rainer Maria. *Sonnets to Orpheus.* Bilingual edition, translated by M. D. Herter Norton. New York: Norton, 1962.

Weber, Samuel M. *Rückkehr zu Freud. Jacques Lacan's Entstellung der Psychoanalyse.* Frankfurt: Ullstein, 1978.

Index